My Character Wouldn't Do That

T0348072

My Character Wouldn't Do That

Acting, Cognitive Science and the Optimal Performance Brain

DONNA SOTO-MORETTINI

methuen | drama

LONDON • NEW YORK • OXFORD • NEW DELHI • SYDNEY

METHUEN DRAMA
Bloomsbury Publishing Plc
50 Bedford Square, London, WC1B 3DP, UK
1385 Broadway, New York, NY 10018, USA
29 Earlsfort Terrace, Dublin 2, Ireland

BLOOMSBURY, METHUEN DRAMA and the Methuen Drama logo
are trademarks of Bloomsbury Publishing Plc

First published in Great Britain 2022

Cover design by Ben Anslow
Cover images: Black woman raising her eyebrow (© Ariel Skelley /
Getty Images); Woman crying (© Cultura RM / Alamy); Man shouting
(© Tara Moore / Getty Images); Young man laughing (© Tara Moore / Getty
Images); Shocked young woman (© Izusek / Getty Images); Portrait of
a man with a quizzical expression (© We Are / Getty Images)

A catalogue record for this book is available from the British Library.

A catalog record for this book is available from the Library of Congress.

ISBN: HB: 978-1-3502-3035-4
       PB: 978-1-3502-3034-7
       ePDF: 978-1-3502-3036-1
       eBook: 978-1-3502-3037-8

Typeset by Integra Software Services Pvt. Ltd.

To find out more about our authors and books visit www.bloomsbury.com
and sign up for our newsletters.

Contents

Acknowledgements

In my working life, I have often been blessed with great colleagues, but none more so than my current colleagues, Iain Davie and Ian Dunn, whose support at all times is greatly appreciated. Thanks also to my students (who so often provide the feedback for my more left -of-centre ideas), and to Rita McAllister and Lise Olson who listen so patiently to my endless rehearsals of thought while writing. From Bloomsbury I want to thank Meredith Benson, whose encouragement transformed my intention into action, and also Anna Brewer and Sam Nicholls for their help along the way. A special thanks for her generosity to Annie Murphy Paul.

Introduction

What this book is

I once had a professor who taught acting at the University of California many years ago who had an extraordinary disdain for acting books. It was his view that Stanislavski had written all that could be written and that everything else to follow was just a rehash of the great man's work. I cannot imagine this was a popular opinion amongst his peers, at least one of whom had written a couple of books on acting.

Nevertheless, he told us one day that people who write acting books were, in his view, on an ethical level with people who ran pay toilets. Both, he said, preyed on human desperation.

So it is with some trepidation that I start this book. It isn't that I haven't written about acting before. But my previous books were looking at very specific areas. They focused on things like auditioning or coping with Shakespeare's text, or looking in a more philosophical way at the kind of language we use when we talk about acting. As a writer, my guiding principle has always been never to spend good time doing something that someone else has done well, and I hope that these earlier books were unique in their approach.

Similarly, I hope that this one is too. But with the words of my old professor ringing in my ears, I have to face the fact that this is a book about acting. Perhaps you can imagine, then, why I am keen to explain right from the start why this book is so different from any other acting books you may have read.

First, it is not meant to replace other books. Instead, it is meant to function as a kind of companion to other books on acting. There are a lot of interesting and varied approaches to the art of acting and most actors I know (or have taught) seem to have some favourites that have worked well for them. You should be able to use this book alongside any others that you have found helpful, and which probably address acting in more traditional ways. This means that the book does not aim to offer a lot of practical acting tips – instead it aims to help you get into the right mental space for acting.

Second, it uses contemporary research in a wide range of other disciplines like cognitive science, cognitive psychology, social psychology and sports psychology to explore what it is that underpins the creation of an acting performance and focuses particularly on what is going on in our brain/mind when we are acting or preparing for performance.

Third, it looks very closely at areas that have not been addressed at a more fundamental level in acting books. We are not just going to assume that when we talk about abstract concepts like imagination or focus that we KNOW what we are talking about. Our minds are incredibly complex, and I am convinced that it will help your work as an actor to know a little more about that complexity.

Finally, it looks at how you can apply that deeper knowledge to your work in very practical ways. Knowing more about how your mind works means that you can employ memory, or focus or imagination in ways that will support your performance rather than distract from it.

My first aim in writing this book is to unravel some of the complexity of concepts we use when acting. We talk about imagination as if we all know what that means and as if there is only one thing we are referring to when we talk about it in practical terms. We talk about emotion as if we know what that is, and how it is generated. We talk about memory as if everyone just knows how to work it. My aim here is to unpack the complexity in these areas and to make our thinking and our language more precise. So we will be looking more closely at how different kinds of imaginings work, at why emotion is *not* feeling, at how we can work *with* our memory instead of *against* it and at why character may be neither stable nor known to ourselves.

My second aim in writing is to tackle head on what I believe to be the greatest struggle facing most actors, and that is the battle against self-consciousness in performance. I hope that by the end of this book you will have a better understanding of the ways in which our battle to stay focused in the present moment while we perform can be disrupted by the ways in which we learn, and by the ways in which we think about our relationship (both as actors and as people) to the world around us.

What this book is NOT

This book is not, in any traditional sense, an academic book. While it rests on much research, what I am presenting is a practical book that focuses on how research carried out in a variety of academic disciplines can illuminate and strengthen our work as actors by helping us create the right mental space for that work. There are several good academic books that look more closely at the theory behind what I present here, and if you want to read some traditional academic scholarship in any of the areas we cover here, I've included an extensive list of resources at the end that will help you find that work.

The structure of this book

My first thought was to structure the book in the three stages of an actor's work: research/preparation, rehearsal and performance. But I learned quickly that this was impossible. Because before I can do that, I must make something *explicit* that I think has only ever been *implicit* in acting (either the practice or in the books written about that practice), which is the fundamental fact that an actor's work must happen in the three very distinct stages listed above: research/ preparation, rehearsal and performance.

These stages are distinct because in each stage, we are in fact using different modes of thinking, different kinds of imagination, and different kinds of memory.

This means I cannot talk about these stages without having looked first at how the different modes of thinking, memory and imagination interact with the actor's brain in each stage. But before we get to that we need to think a moment about what makes a good acting performance, and what makes a bad one.

Acting: good and bad

Good acting displays infinite variety. For that reason, people often argue over an acting performance: what works for one person might not for another. Good acting comes in many guises – one may find it in the glorious excesses of actors like David Tennant, Peter O'Toole or Vanessa Redgrave. Some may find it in the mannerisms of Alan Rickman, Maggie Smith or Jack Nicholson. For many, it can be found in the considered restraint of Anthony Hopkins or John Gielgud. It might have the intellectual qualities of Benedict Cumberbatch or Meryl Streep, or the homely qualities of Julie Walters or Tom Hanks. Some good actors dazzle us with transformational abilities and some with their ability to 'remain themselves' from role to role, and yet somehow convince us that we have seen the deep inner workings of a soul. Some surprise us, some frighten us, some seem great because of their intensity, some because of their ease. Some have an uncanny knack of simulating (or feeling?) emotion, and some avoid emotional display altogether and yet still manage to make us believe that they have revealed much about themselves.

Perhaps because its manifestations are quite so various, describing good acting can be incredibly challenging, and while there may be those who can speak with knowledge or experience about the technique of acting in their consideration of a performance, the great majority of people in any given audience are content to say that they may not know what constitutes great acting, but they know what they like.

Bad acting, I would suggest, has far less variety to consider and for that reason I believe that it rewards some contemplation. I believe that almost all bad acting has one thing in common: interference from the performer's self-consciousness. We can sense a performer's self-consciousness in several ways: it might be that we can see a performer stiffening up physically out of fear and lacking natural ease, we might sense that they are limiting their immediate responses or worrying about being watched/judged. We might sense that self-consciousness in the way that the actor appears to be judging themselves or their character as they go along. We might sense that self-consciousness in the actors' desire to be noticed, or to get laughs. We might feel that the actor has little sense of belief in what they are saying, or little sense of belief that the scene they find themselves in is real. And sometimes we might be aware that there is a kind of mental battle that is compromising the actor's ability to inhabit a scene spontaneously and to be responsive 'in the moment'. There are, then, various manifestations of self-consciousness in an actor, but all self-conscious acting is bad acting, and it can leave both actor and viewer uncomfortable.

If you are reading this as an actor of some experience, you probably recognize the way that when we feel our own performance has been good, we have the sense that our imagination 'clicked' with the other performers, with the environment and with the story. Our performances 'click' when our imagination and attention are so strong that we find it easy to pretend that what is happening is 'real'. That 'real' must be in inverted commas, because even when the imagination and attention are marshalled brilliantly, even when the pretence seems palpable, some part of our mind must know that Othello isn't *really* going to kill us.

If you are a performer of some experience (even if only acting in classroom situations), you probably also recognize the ways in which self-consciousness seems to kill all the pleasure in work. What we want to do when we act is to engage in an imagined environment in the most un-self-conscious way possible. I think that if you want to teach someone to be a successful actor you must start with this idea first. The basic argument of this book is that self-consciousness is – amongst other things – the common factor in nearly all bad acting.

Following on from that argument, one of my primary concerns here will be entirely about how we can minimize self-consciousness when acting. In order to do that I need to look at a lot of areas that traditional acting books haven't. This is because science has moved on quite a bit since the first books on acting theory were written. And in that time, a lot has been learned about the brain and how it works. I am going to be drawing on that kind of research to rethink some of the things that we do as actors and as teachers/directors of actors. Because the variety of great acting is too wide to be contained within a book, and the many approaches to creating great performance can't be captured in a single system or idea, one the main aims of this book will be to look at ways in which actors can minimize self-consciousness and work in a more pleasurable way.

What does a good acting performance feel like?

My guess is that you do one of your best acting performances off stage. And to explain this, I want to start with a question: when do you talk to yourself, and what do you say?

I always ask this question of actors when they are preparing a monologue or a soliloquy and are wondering why I tell them repeatedly that an actor must NEVER be talking to themselves. So let's think about that question: when do you talk to yourself, and what do you say? The memories that invariably emerge when I ask are always of a kind of low energy, barely-spoken-out-loud set of questions or self-reprimands, like 'where are my keys?' or 'why does my hair look so horrible?' or 'you're going to be late!' We generally agree that we are not the kindest people when we talk to ourselves and that we habitually give ourselves a hard time. I then remind them that there is one situation when they talk at a point where there is no one around, and that situation is when they are:

1. Rehearsing an argument or conversation they are about to have.

2. Replaying an argument or conversation they have just had, but this time they say all the things they *meant* to say.

Always, at this point, people generally smile or laugh in recognition of something that I have now concluded must be a universal 'secret' activity. I have never encountered an actor (or indeed anyone!) who has not done this kind of 'bedroom' pre-argument performance. When I ask them what really distinguishes this kind of talking on your own from the other kind of talking to themselves ('where did I put my keys?'), the answers are very much about the way in which rehearsing or replaying an argument takes a lot of concentration and intention. It is easy to talk to yourself about finding your keys, but it takes some focus and energy to rehearse an important argument or an important emotional revelation. They know (and can see in their minds):

- exactly who it is they are talking to and how that person sees them at the moment;

- what they think that person is likely to say;

- exactly what they want from this argument and what the ideal outcome is;

- what they want the person they're imagining to feel at the end of this exchange;

- and what has to change and how they're going to change it.

This kind of 'rehearsed argument' activity is a great example of the brain in task-oriented, present-thinking mode, which is where we need to be when acting. All the actors when asked will say that they were animated, energized and can remember that they were feeling something (usually anger or self-righteousness if arguing or sometimes they remember feeling love or happiness if the conversation is about revealing feelings or of needing more time and attention from someone). But they were not thinking about creating or simulating that emotion/feeling. Those feelings just emerged spontaneously in the course of their task-oriented, specific engagement during which they could deeply imagine who they were talking to and what they wanted to make that person feel and how they wanted that person to see them at the end of the exchange.

Students all generally agree that while having this rehearsal/replay argument/conversation, they recall no sense whatever of self-consciousness, and instead remember just being focused in the moment of the 'exchange'.

For me, this is the description of good acting. Not GREAT acting perhaps, because GREAT acting might require much more in terms of technique, depth, variety, subtlety, range, etc. But it is *good* acting in these terms:

- it is happening in the present;
- it is full of action;
- it is un-self-conscious;
- and whatever emotion/feeling happens, it arises organically and is not generated by the 'actor'.

I think this is how things should work for an actor when they are performing. In the attempt to change what we see in front of us, we engage wholeheartedly with the task.

The job of the actor is to make an audience feel emotionally engaged with a story. This means, by definition, that the job of the actor is to DO things – to take action. While taking that action and interacting with others, the actor's own emotion, or character or self-consciousness should not enter the picture. But is this 'bedroom' pretence really acting?

What is acting?

I tried many years ago to define acting and found it much more difficult than I had expected it to be. After all, I had been a student and then a teacher of acting for decades. Surely there was a quick answer to this question? If I looked in books, I found a lot of ideas framed around the word 'truth'. Acting was certainly related to 'truth' for most authors of books about acting. Acting was also related to 'action'. And to creating a character. And to connecting with emotion. And sometimes to creating a kind of high energy or 'raising the stakes' in a performance. Indeed, there are a lot of things written about acting, but very rarely, I find, do people ever attempt to answer this simple question: *what it is we are doing when we are acting?*

We know that there are a lot of things involved in acting, but we also know that any one of these things alone do not make up the practice we call acting.

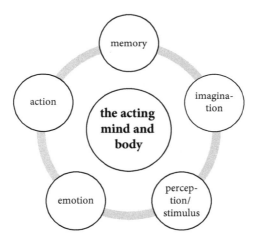

Sanford Meisner once said that acting was living truthfully under imaginary circumstances and I think that is as close as most people get to finding a workable definition of acting. But of course, we know that 'living' is rather ambiguous here – we would be living whether we were acting or not. And using the word 'truth' is always a problem – I have learned many times in audition panels or when sharing a drink after a night at the theatre that what feels 'truthful' to me does not always feel 'truthful' to anyone else!

Perhaps it would be better for us to say that acting is being active under imaginary circumstances. But even with this definition we are left with some interesting questions. Why not just say that acting is pretending that something fictional is real?

Well, that does not quite cover it because I can imagine right now that Lady Macbeth is real, but that does not mean I am acting. In order to act, I must involve my body. I must be doing something *as* Lady Macbeth, and while I am doing that 'something' I have to pretend that the circumstances in which I am doing that something are *real*. So, in this sense, acting always involves a body and some action. I think it is important for us to remember that. And even if we do not like the word 'pretending', acting always involves both our brains and our bodies pretending to do something in fictional circumstances.

But of course, there is more to it than this. In a sense, actors are always pretending on two fronts:

We must work at two kinds of pretending because if we did not KNOW we were pretending, we would probably be having a psychotic episode of some sort! And if we DO know we are pretending, we cannot dwell there in our minds. We must pretend that we are not pretending. I think this happens naturally when we stage our 'bedroom' arguments.

'*Theatrical* pretense: Tom Hanks yells at a volleyball. Why? He is pretending to lose his mind, during the filming of *Castaway*. He is not trying to make anyone believe that he, Tom Hanks, is losing his mind. Nor is he trying to make anyone believe that some other person is losing his mind. The intended audience will know it is just a movie. So this is not a case of deceptive pretense. There is no attempt to give anyone a false belief. At the same time, he has gone well beyond what we would normally call "make-believe." He is entirely serious in this endeavour and will be (more than) amply compensated.'[1]

---

[1] Langland-Hassan (2014).

The longer I teach, the more certain I am that each actor experiences the practice differently, and each actor brings their own keys to the mystery of sustaining a pretence over three or five acts. But however differently they may practise, I think most actors can improve their performance by understanding how the brain works in the preparation, rehearsal and performance stages of the work.

An actor's brain works optimally in three stages

It may sound incredibly obvious – and it does to me while I write this! – but we need to start by acknowledging that the work of creating a performance happens in three very distinct stages. There are two preparation stages and there is a performance stage. If you get the preparation stages right, you will almost certainly have a much easier time keeping your thoughts focused outward in the performance stage. In fact, *unless* you get that preparation stage right, you do not really have a chance of remaining focused on the world around you as you perform. And once you have done the work on preparation, you must trust that what happens in those first two stages is going to stay with you in performance.

As critical as it is to see that the brain works differently in the rehearsal/preparation stage than it does in the performance stage, there appears to be very little written about this. I have come to think that the reason so many of the young actors I work with bring so much unwanted thought into performance is that the books they have read and the training that they've done previously don't seem to emphasize in a very clear way how important it is for actors to keep the tasks/thoughts required for preparation work separate from the tasks/ thoughts required for performance work. I do think this idea is *implied* in almost any acting book you read, but if I judge just by what I see when training young actors, I don't think the importance of this idea has been made explicit enough.

Perhaps one of the most important things an actor can learn is to know when performance IS performance and not just another stage in the learning process.

Performance is a demonstration of the ability to focus on and sustain (for the length of a play/scene) our engagement in an imagined world.

Everything else – trying to remember lines, monitoring the process of creating a convincing dialect, remembering what the director said – **is part of the preparation and rehearsal process**. In the following chapters we will be looking very closely at how our brains work in these different stages.

We will be considering a lot of things to do with brain and body function, and I will also, throughout this book, be suggesting that it is time for us to rethink things like character, subconscious drives or motivations, self-knowledge, self-related thought, imagination, the generation of emotions and thought and how all of these things operate in relation to our work as actors. Because if we are in the business of simulating 'believable' human behaviour, we can surely only be helped by a deeper understanding of how human behaviour is generated in the first place.

Acting is a holistic process

And herein lies one of the difficulties in writing a book like this. Acting is a process that involves us in many things at once: imagination, memory, action, physicality and any other incidental things that might be required of us in order to be convincing. But I can only address these things here in an orderly way. That means there will be chapters on thinking, emotion, character, memory but we do not experience these things separately as actors. So what follows is a taking apart – a 'disaggregation' of the normally synchronous experience of thinking, moving, talking and remembering that makes up our practical work. And as much as I have tried to take these things apart, they inevitably overlap at various points.

The actor's brain

We start by thinking. What shall we think about? And how will we do it? Who does the thinking for you? It is common to think that our thinking is carried out in our brains. We tend to have a view of the brain that is kind of like a computer. We often imagine that if we need to solve a problem it simply gets solved by the 'computer' in our heads, and then we carry out a solution. But increasingly, cognitive scientists – and particularly artificial intelligence designers – are learning that thinking is generated differently: that we 'think' outside our brains, and in a more cyclical way.

If we consider the computer model of the brain, we might imagine that there is a kind of linear process to thinking:

1. we sense

2. we think

3. we act.

But what we are learning is that our thinking processes – cognition – is embodied. In other words, our bodies are part of the process. This is a complicated area, but I think there are some easy ways to access some of the importance of the body in our cognitive processes.

For example, our bodies often know what is going on before our brains have time to process. You may have experienced this if you have ever been expecting a letter or an email following an important application or interview that you were really excited about. For example, imagine you have auditioned for a film, and you really want the part. You look at your phone and see that there is a message from your agent. Almost invariably you feel something very definitely and very quickly in your body at the simple sight of the message. You do not know what that message is, but your body recognizes instantly that this is something that will affect you significantly and it registers that knowledge powerfully before you have the chance to think about it.

Along with impulses and thoughts generated by our bodies, we can experience the same from the world around us. It is common these days to talk about 'trigger' warnings, which are a good example of the way that external happenings can induce memory or thought. Victims of PTSD often refer to the way that experiences can 'trigger' a memory out of the blue and often in ways they do not even understand. Of course, we are thinking about these things once they have been 'triggered', but these provide an example of the way in which thought is not always generated consciously by our 'computer brains'.

In a now well-known article called *The Extended Mind*, Andy Clark and David Chalmers ask 'Where does the mind stop, and the rest of the world begin?' They argue that our environment plays an active role in driving our thinking processes.

I'm beginning this chapter with a short meditation on the extended mind, or 'embodied cognition' as it is more commonly known, because I think actors can benefit from thinking more about how thought is extended into environment, is generated with and through our bodies and is not solely the result of our brains performing computer functions.

Our specs

Wherever it is that thought is generated, and however extended our minds may be in their various processes, it is certainly true that our brains have a limit to the information that they can process at any given time. If we did think of our brains as computers, just what are our specs? Well, in acting terms they certainly have their limits.

In an average production, the actor is almost always:

1.   Retrieving text from memory – sometimes a very great deal
     of text. Hamlet, for example, speaks 30,557 words, or about
     one-third of the average novel.

2.   Remembering specific technical things (find your light/
     remember that we re-blocked the end of this scene, exit
     downstage left, etc.).

3.   Straddling a number of different time frames: *the past* (a
     long-term memory of everything rehearsed including all
     physical and technical details); *the present* (being 'connected'
     or 'in the moment' so that the actor seems to be responding
     spontaneously to what is happening on stage); and *the
     future* (anticipating what will or what may happen and being
     prepared for that).

4.   Along with all this most actors are taught to carry a kind of
     'thought process' in their heads such as:

Hamlet: (*it's now or never. We're finally alone*) Where's your father?
(*I have to know if she loves me enough to tell me the truth*)

Brain researchers Rene Marois and Jason Ivanoff explain: 'The human brain is heralded for its staggering complexity and processing capacity: its hundred billion (10th to 11th power) neurons and several hundred trillion synaptic connections can process and exchange prodigious amounts of information over a distributed neural network in the matter of milliseconds. Such massive parallel processing capacity permits our visual system to successfully decode complex images in 100 ms, and our brain to store upwards of 109 bits of information over our lifetime, more than 50,000 times the text contained in the US Library of Congress. Yet, for all our neurocomputational sophistication and processing power, we can barely attend to more than one object at a time, and we can hardly perform two tasks at once.'[1]

---

[1] Marois and Ivanoff (2005).

In other words, *we have to be economic when we decide what to spend our limited cognitive resources on.* That means the more information an actor can pass into an 'automatic' state – which we don't have to expend effort to retrieve – the more working space we have for focusing on and interacting with the world around us and the less cognitive load we carry.

But knowing just how limited our working cognitive space is should also make us realize how important it is to prioritize in terms of what we use that limited cognitive working space for. We want to use that cognitive working space to imagine in full detail the world we are pretending to inhabit. We want to be able to react in a spontaneous way to what is happening around us, we want to surprise, engage and get what we want from those we are sharing the stage with. We want to be concentrating on what they're doing/what they're thinking about us, we want to have the mental space to notice the small changes that happen that might indicate what is really going on their minds.

Of the four tasks listed above, the one that often adds the most the actor's cognitive load is number 1: the text retrieval, and if we are not prepared well enough it IS the most demanding. But if we get our preparation right, that part is surprisingly undemanding and instead, numbers 2 and 4 take up the space.

But when we do not get the preparation right, the fight for cognitive space can turn into an uncomfortable internal battle.

Battling on more than one front

As we noted in the Introduction, one of the hallmarks of bad acting is self-consciousness. This is a problem for most actors at some point in their careers, and it feels like a very separate problem from simply considering the limit of information we can deal with at any one time. But of course, it is not entirely separate, because self-conscious thought takes up precious cognitive space. So it is worth taking a bit of time here to consider self-consciousness: what it is and whether we can ever defeat it while we are performing.

In neuroscientific/psychological terms, self-consciousness is part of self-related thought, which is a very large category that includes the regulation of our bodily needs/functions, or of how we construct a sense of ourselves through time, or perhaps how we distinguish between that 'historical' sense of self, and the self that is immediately perceiving the world around us. Much of this thought is unconscious.

For our purposes, we are interested in the kind of conscious self-related thought that occurs when we are being watched, and in how being watched affects our sense of ourselves and our behaviour. For some psychologists, self-consciousness is entirely constructed by imagining how others see us. Most of us have known the fear of being judged by others for how we look or how we behave, and we know how powerful that fear can be in shaping our choices sometimes. Because acting always involves being watched and being judged, it can raise some powerful fear responses in us as we perform. This fear is driven by a social need – there is a kind of hard-wired design in human beings to seek acceptance and approval, and it has been argued that this need for approval has been increased by engaging on social media platforms like Twitter or Instagram, which can have a negative influence on our sense of well-being.

But psychologist Charles Carver focuses not on the way in which we imagine how others see us but into the ways in which we monitor and judge ourselves. He has developed a set of self-assessment questions that can help people determine (or even just think more specifically about) how much they expect from themselves:

1. Compared to other people, I expect a lot from myself.

2. When even one thing goes wrong I begin to wonder if I can do well at anything at all.

3. I get angry with myself if my efforts don't lead to the results I wanted.

4. When it comes to setting standards for my behaviour, I aim higher than most people.

5. I hardly ever let unhappiness over one bad time influence my feelings about other parts of my life.

6. When I don't do as well as I hoped to, I often get upset with myself.

7. I set higher goals for myself than other people seem to.

8. If I notice one fault of mine, it makes me think about my other faults.

9. I get unhappy with anything less than what I expected of myself.

10. A single failure can change me from feeling OK to seeing only the bad in myself.

Answer scale:
  1 = I agree a lot
  2 = I agree a little
  3 = I'm in the middle – I neither agree nor disagree
  4 = I DISagree a little
  5 = I DISagree a lot[2]

In Carver's view, if you agreed with most of the questions except number 5, it is likely that your strong expectations of yourself may contribute to self-consciousness, since the pressure of your own expectations may lead you to monitor yourself more closely.

Whether self-consciousness comes from giving ourselves a hard time, or worrying about what others think, we know that it takes up valuable space in our heads. And we know that it engenders fear. Often it evokes the kind of fear that makes us unwilling to play, to take risks or to enjoy the possibility of getting it completely wrong. When it does that, we lose not only the joy of performing, but we become rather dull as well.

How is self-consciousness related to fear

Extreme self-awareness in social situations is a form of anxiety and in some cases connected to neurosis. One might not expect to

---

[2]Carver makes this test free and you can access it from the Department of Psychology pages on the University of Miami website, https://local.psy.miami.edu/people/faculty/ccarver/available-self-report-instruments/ats/.

encounter people who are deeply self-conscious to be in an acting class, but in fact I encounter them regularly. And when I look back on my experience as a performer, I would have to place myself in this category. Some can learn to redirect their attention well enough to overcome that self-awareness and some cannot.

The ones who cannot are precisely those I described at the opening of the book: you can sense their self-awareness and it makes both actor and audience uncomfortable. When I watch these kinds of actors in the early stages of classes, their response to being watched is most often manifest in their bodies: an observable stiffness or lack of ease, or a kind of 'frozen' body. At other times I can hear it in their voices, as the usual ease and natural 'melody' of the spoken sound becomes rather flat with limited intonation and a kind of 'stiff' delivery. After watching extremely self-conscious performances, I always ask the actor what they can remember of what they were thinking. Four answers are common, and all of them pull the actor away from the central task they are meant to be concentrating on:

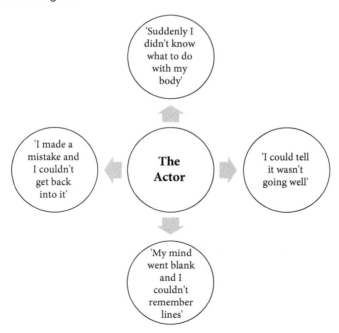

Most of these are easy to understand, and it is easy to see why they knock you out of an effective performance mode. But why are these kinds of thoughts so common?

'Suddenly I didn't know what to do with my body'

If I ask you to think right now about what you usually do with your hands when you are talking to your best friend, you probably could not tell me. That is because when you are talking to your best friend you are not thinking about your hands. And when you *do* think about your hands, you suddenly forget what you usually do with them.

When actors don't know what to do with their bodies, they're thinking about their bodies in ways that don't come naturally to them. It is the same reason some of us find it hard to smile or pose with ease in front of a camera – suddenly we know we're being watched and that the way we look in a photo is a permanent record that many people might see. That is a pretty scary thought, and that makes us think about things we don't normally ever think about (*how do I look? How do I usually smile? What do I do with my hands?*). Thinking about things (particularly physical movement things) we don't need to think about can be as big a problem for athletes as it is for actors. It is one thing to be unsure of just how to smile for the camera, but another thing altogether to be unsure about what you need to do to produce your best backhand shot at Wimbledon. But the effects of thinking about your movement can be as devastating for an actor's performance as it is for an athlete's.

Researchers in this area call thinking about movement you have already mastered 'reinvestment' – meaning that we 'reinvest' time thinking about automatic behaviour in the hope that such thinking can be of use in making a performance better ('Perhaps I'll just cross my arms and I'll look natural ... ').[3] But in fact, once a skill has passed into 'automatic' phase (which is where a great tennis player's backhand return – or an actor's performance – should be), reinvesting time in that thinking process quickly disrupts the skill. If you are a piano player or a touch typist, you will know what thinking about your fingers as

---

[3]Masters and Maxwell (2008).

you play or type will do to your playing or your typing! So thinking about your body or your lines when performing results in damaging self-consciousness, and thinking about the process of performance while performing will disrupt performance.

An influential article puts this well: 'Under pressure, a person realizes consciously that it is important to execute behaviour correctly [so] consciousness attempts to ensure the correctness by monitoring the process ... But consciousness does not contain the knowledge of these skills.'[4] That seems surprising, doesn't it? Surely consciousness is where such knowledge resides? Well, in the case of well-learned skill (things like lines, how your body moves naturally, scene blocking, what is happening on stage), such knowledge will have passed into the 'automatic' part of your memory, and that part of your memory does not reside in the thinking part of your brain. So consciously monitoring what you have learned to the automatic phase will disturb the ease and flow of execution. And likewise, thinking about how to smile or move your hands will seriously disrupt your ability to smile or move your hands with a natural ease.

'My mind went blank'

Worrying about how we move our hands or bodies is only one type of self-conscious thinking that can affect an acting performance. Often we freeze up when we're thinking about our minds – especially in terms of retrieving lost text. This can make our minds go blank, and then we must direct effort (either successfully or unsuccessfully) to remember lines. Of course, a blank or panicking mind also knocks us out of performance mode. Sometimes our minds can go blank if we get into a state where fear takes over. The source of that fear could be many things.

We have considered the ways in which others watching/judging us, or judging ourselves contributes to fear. But it could also be that a performance is under-rehearsed, the actor may feel insecure about the text, or perhaps it is just a particularly challenging scene. But almost always, actors know that being watched equals being judged, and that alone can make us fearful.

---

[4]Baumeister (1984).

Fear has a powerful influence on the way our brains work, and that is because it is a significant factor in the way we are designed to survive. When we are in a dangerous situation, we do not have time to think, so a strong fear response suppresses our usual thinking apparatus. The stronger the fear, the less we can think clearly. Instead of stopping to consider, our brain is preparing our bodies to fight or to flee.

It is extraordinary to think that presenting a scene from *The Importance of Being Ernest* can kick in a fear response from us that was designed to save us from being eaten by a sabre-toothed cat. But if you have ever found your heart racing/pounding, your palms sweaty, your mouth dry, your face flushed or your head going a bit blank and fuzzy before you get up to give us your Lady Bracknell, then you will recognize the physical indicators of the 'fear response'. There are many reasons why actors might feel such a powerful fear instinct kick in, and no doubt many unknown reasons why some actors have a greater fear response than others. But the strange fact is that the physical symptoms you undergo in an acting class or performance are the same ones designed to prepare your body either to run for or to fight for your life.

'I could tell it wasn't going well'

When an actor says that they knew their performance was not going well, or that they made a mistake and then couldn't get back into the swing of the performance, they are basically saying that in the middle of their performance, they left the present and returned to the past. In the first instance, they are remembering a rehearsal that they liked, and that means they could not stay in the present. In the second instance, they were going over a mistake that had already happened – and once again, they were not able to stay in the present. For an actor, the only place we can be effective is in the present, while aiming for a desired future.

The Past	The Present	The Future
• how it worked in rehearsal • how I said that line before when I liked the sound of it	• what I see/hear • what I do	• my ideal outcome

When we are performing, the future only matters in the present because it influences how we play our actions. But when the past invades, the outcome is nearly always deadly. Fear, thinking about ourselves and how we are seen and dwelling in the past are all powerful stressors during a performance and they take us out of the optimum mind space we need for achieving creative work and performing excellence.

Fear and risk

At the very core of creativity is risk. As actors we are often told to risk more; to be bolder in our work. But the fear of being judged tends to make us risk averse. This is a serious obstacle on the path of improving our performance. Great performances require freedom, flexibility, openness, bold choices and secure imaginative connection to all around us. But of course, fear creates caution, timidity, limited range and choice, and a performer locked in mental battle with themselves. So how do we prepare ourselves to win this battle? One important key lies in understanding the kinds of mental states – or 'brain modes' – we need to employ as we work through the stages of preparation, rehearsal and performance.

Understanding modes of thinking

Brains seem to have many modes and we need to focus on two. The first is what has come to be known as 'default mode' – which is the mode of thought that comes into action when we are not focused on any goal-oriented task. It is sometimes referred to as 'the daydreaming' mode. In other words, when we do not have something that demands our attention in a specific way (or perhaps demands that we do something, or make decisions about what to do), our brains tend to revert to what has been called 'default mode'. There are some controversial debates amongst neuroscientists about exactly what brain areas and networks are involved in default mode but I think in a very common sense way we can recognize what is being referred to when I describe default brain mode, and basically it looks like this:

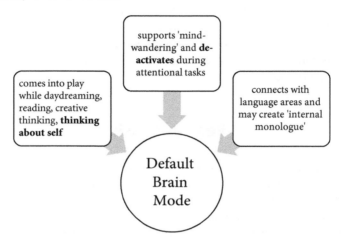

comes into play while daydreaming, reading, creative thinking, **thinking about self**

supports 'mind-wandering' and **de-activates** during attentional tasks

connects with language areas and may create 'internal monologue'

Default Brain Mode

The default mode is complex, and it is involved in many things that the brain does, but all an actor needs to know about it is that it is the mode that we engage when we are not focusing on anything demanding. It is what we use when we are sort of wandering around mentally, perhaps daydreaming, or thinking about ourselves. It kicks in when we are reading or remembering things from the past, and it is involved when we are considering anything autobiographical or anything beautiful. It has tasks, of course, because just remembering how we felt last summer is a task of sorts. But it is not the sharply focused brain mode we engage when we are involved in something that demands that we pay full attention. If you have ever tried to meditate, you will almost certainly recognize default mode, as this is the mode employed when your mind just drifts and chatters away to itself, and most meditators must work hard to suppress that chatter. It is a rather internal mode of thinking, although certainly it takes in the outside world.

One of the distinguishing traits of the default mode is its quick (and sometimes almost random) associative thought process. This is why, when our minds are wandering it is extraordinary how quickly we can flit from thought to thought. I once studied with a meditation teacher who described the 'chattering brain' as 'lurching like a drunken monkey' from one thing to the next. The random, lateral, free-association nature of the default brain is what makes this mode of thinking so valuable for creativity, innovation and problem-solving.

The second mode of thought is sometimes referred to as task-oriented or 'task-positive' thought. This kind of thinking is just what it sounds like: it is the way your brain performs when you need to marshal your attention and get something done. Task-positive mode could also be thought of as an externally focused mode, since it generally involves getting things done in the world around you. It stays focused and in this state your attention can often feel so focused that you lose track of time. If default mode is where we *create* choices, task-positive mode is where we *make* choices.

In these two states, if you were to study a functional MRI picture of each closely, you would see that very different areas of the brain light up, depending on which mode of thought you were engaging, as they use different networks of neurons in the brain.

Default Mode Network
more active at rest (task-negative)
mind wandering

Attention Network
more active during tasks (task-positive)
engaged attention

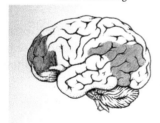 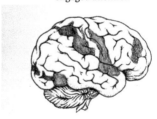

If you think about these two modes of thinking from the point of view of an actor, it should come as no surprise that for performance, the mode required is task-positive thought mode. And most acting books from Stanislavski onward have extolled the importance of finding objectives or actions that actors can pursue in a scene. Finding and focusing on objectives keeps us actively involved in the world around us and prevents us from slipping into 'default mode', which is where self-conscious thinking resides. In default mode we exhibit less interest in what is going on around us and our energy (in terms of being involved in the world around us) drops as well. So task-positive mode in performance it is then.

This makes the advice to actors – from Stanislavski to Declan Donellan – about focusing on objectives make so much sense. Stanislavski spoke of objectives and super-objectives. Declan Donnellan talks about 'the target' but both, writing some seventy or eighty years apart, are aware of the importance of actors remaining focused on the world outside themselves.

The paradox of control

It is all very well saying that we want to avoid self-consciousness in performance, or we want to be in task-mode and not in default mode when we are performing, but there is an extraordinary paradox for us to consider here: often the more we try to control our brains, the less control we have. Trying to control our thoughts often leads us to thinking about exactly the thing we were trying not the think of. The same is true of behaviour. Think for a moment about how hard it is to go to sleep when you are trying to make yourself go to sleep, or how difficult it is not to think of food when you are on a diet, or to stop thinking about someone you are angry with.

Similarly, we cannot *make* ourselves switch out of default brain mode; instead we want to create the conditions in which it can happen. Actors have two difficulties in this area. First, we are often thinking that we must control our behaviour on stage:

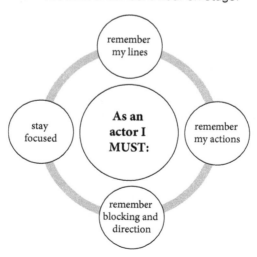

Second, while we are doing all this, we are also thinking we have to control or direct our imaginations in such a way that what is happening seems spontaneous and utterly believed. That is a lot of work, and it is also a lot for us to be trying to control while looking 'natural' and at ease.

The paradox, of course, is that the more we try to control all of this, the more self-related our thought becomes. And research has shown that we are only going to really escape the self-related thought if we can enter into a state called 'hypo-egoic', in which we learn to relinquish control of our thoughts.

Hypo-what?

Hypo-egoic is not as complex as it sounds – it simply means 'underneath' the ego, and it is at the heart of the paradox mentioned earlier. It means that to perform well, we have to give up the idea of consciously controlling everything. Instead, we need to find a way to sit 'underneath' the ego and its desire to control everything. If we can do that, we can use that freed up 'controlling' area of the brain to make decisions about what to do when things are happening to us (and around us) in performance and the present moment.

Clearly this is a thin line: we do of course want to make decisions – actors and directors talk all the time about making effective choices – and we do want to affect the world around us when we are on stage. But importantly, much of the performance work *has to be spontaneous*, and that is only going to happen when we're *not* caught up in trying to control our behaviours while we perform. We considered this earlier, when thinking about the desire (under pressure) to monitor the process of performance rather than just performing. This idea becomes clearer when you think of a great concert pianist. Every great concert musician begins by thinking about and controlling the processes involved in performance:

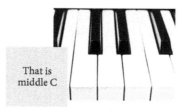

'I hold my hands this way'
'This section is quiet'
'That is middle C'

This kind of thinking, monitoring and controlling can and *must* happen while learning and practising. Once the pianist is performing in concert, however, they absolutely MUST NOT be thinking any of these things.

Image credit: Shutterstock.

To do so is to engage in the kind of thought we considered earlier: 'reinvesting'. If the concert pianist 'reinvests' time thinking about how to hold her hands, or which fingers to use, she will knock herself out of the 'flow' state required to give a great performance. And the truth is, if she is still at a point where she *needs* to be thinking about how to hold her hands or which fingers to use, she is not ready to be performing. At the point of performance we hope to be in that hypo-egoic state: allowing what we've learned securely to run the show without us thinking about it. We want to give up the sense of having to control and instead, enjoy the sense of allowing things to happen.

Divergent, lateral and convergent thinking

Actors use both divergent and convergent thinking over the course of their process in building a performance. It is helpful to think for a moment about the difference in these kinds of thinking, because all too often in the early stages of preparation and rehearsal, I think actors rely more than they should on convergent thinking.

Divergent thinking moves outward into diverse possibilities. It starts from a given point and then radiates outward into a lot of ideas:

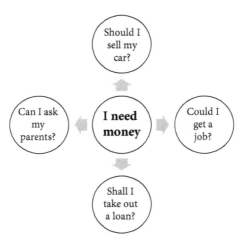

Convergent thinking moves from possibilities to a solution or an answer:

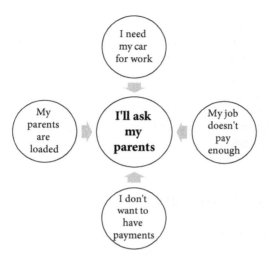

Lateral thinking tends to reframe the proposition altogether or come at it from an unexpected direction:

Divergent thinking is what we use when we are creating a lot of different choices to take into rehearsal. As we explore and experiment we want to move more toward convergent thinking. Actors should be using all of these types of thinking in preparation and remain open to possibilities even when we are in the late stages of rehearsal. Perhaps the bravest among us would say that it is good to keep divergent possibilities in view even in performance mode.

Fluid and crystallized intelligence

Crystallized intelligence is the accumulation of things like knowledge, facts and skills. This is the mind's 'storehouse' of goods and weapons for use in a variety of contexts. Fluid intelligence is the kind of intelligence we use to reason and to cope with the unexpected or the unknown. Fluid intelligence is all about flexibility, problem-solving and meeting with new situations.

Actors use both. We spend time in preparation and rehearsal stages building a powerful store of knowledge, facts and skills that will inform our practice in rehearsals and our ease in the imagined world of performance. In that performance we will also be using fluid intelligence as we remain open to all that goes on around us and can respond flexibly if anything changes in either small or large (dropped lines, missed entrances!) ways.

You can't take preparation into performance

This seems obvious, but I have worked with enough actors in my time to know that it is not. So often the mental battles I watch actors fighting in performance occur because the kind of thinking that is appropriate to preparation and rehearsal is not the kind of thinking you can bring into performance.

It is common for actors to be confused over this. I have watched many training actors perform when they are still trying to retrieve lines, or still trying think about what to do or how to move. But in truth, acting is no different from performing as a musician or an athlete. As an actor, you need to be in the state where you are NOT still thinking about how to move or working to remember a line.

We need to start thinking more like musicians and athletes in this sense. We need to be at a point in our performance where we are not 'reinvesting' time in things that we should have worked out already. Instead, we want to be in a 'flow' state. Flow (which we will be looking more closely at later) is the state that we get into when we are totally immersed in what we are doing. Most people know this state – it happens naturally when we are so involved in doing something that time just seems to fly by. Self-conscious thought is dampened down, and we have a deep sense of concentration. We cannot make ourselves get into flow state – flow is something that happens to us when the external world engages us. For pianists, it is the music, the movement, the sound. For artists it is colour, line, depth. For tennis players it is a challenging opponent. For actors it is playing actions in a demanding imagined world full of risk and reward.

In the right mode at the right time

We have looked now at various kinds of thinking and brain modes, but how can we use this knowledge in the stages of preparation, rehearsal and performance?

Stage one: Cognitive

All the early (preparation) work happens in stage one. In this stage we are largely employing default mode. At this point we are simply reading, considering, thinking and comparing different possibilities available in our approach to a performance. Ideally this would be done both on your own and with partners/ensemble, experimenting with various ideas, researching (style, context or language), perhaps writing (always keep a journal of your process, where you can record research notes, experiences in rehearsal, director's comments). We want to engage our imagination, and that means we want at times to be able to think slowly and in non-linear ways about creative solutions. We also want to consider how our own empathetic/sympathetic responses to character and story will influence choices we may make later. This is the time for you to employ much of the work you glean from acting books and should include things like evaluating your own emotional memory or thoughts about autobiographical resonance with things in the play. It could involve much consideration of visual and musical aspects of the world of the play – gathering a lot of inspiring sources really fuels creative thought. This is the creative learning phase.

At this point we want to employ divergent and lateral thinking, to be exploring widely and creating a lot of resources that we can draw on later. The nature of default mode thinking is that you will often find yourself contemplating ideas that may see odd or counter-intuitive. That is just fine – you want to nurture thoughts like these because acting is an art. And when it comes to art, logic is not your only weapon. Sometimes it is not even your finest weapon.

We should also be building the crystallized intelligence that will inform our work, so this is the time to engage directly with sources (perhaps reading up on nineteenth-century Russian society, learning what you can about life, politics and art of the time) and indirectly using your imagination (take a walk and imagine you are strolling in a wood outside Moscow). In this early stage, try to avoid things like sitting around a table reading with other actors – get up and move together. Getting your body involved early on not only enhances our thinking, we can also learn in indirect ways by experimenting through spontaneous gesture and movement.

For much of this work, we remain in default thinking mode.

Stage two: Associative

This is the rehearsal stage in which we do all the repetition and practice work to embed the creative learning. In this stage you should be comparing what you are currently doing with what you ideally want to be doing – this requires experimentation, exploration and often discussion. At this point you are practising any physical/vocal changes you or your director might think essential for the role, doing all the 'drill' work of encoding and embedding the artistic decisions you and your company have made; in fact every detail of every facet of performance belongs in this stage and your aim is to cement learning by working with repetition (going over scenes and getting used to employing and refining all the detail).

Most of the time, the work in this stage is happening in starts and stops.

This means that when we are in stage two learning, we are switching quickly between task-positive mode and self-aware, default mode.

We try out things in performance and then reflect on their effectiveness. We listen to direction, we apply that direction and then we consider or discuss whether the application of that direction has been effective. We experiment with physical and vocal choices and then analyse them by ourselves or in discussion with others, which means we are using lateral, divergent and convergent thinking.

Experienced actors are incredibly adept at this kind of thought-mode switch and can move swiftly from a discussion about the work (which requires default mode self-reflection) to jumping whole-heartedly back into a performance (which requires task-positive, outwardly directed thought and engagement). All the simultaneous repetition and reflection is encoding and embedding information into our brains. We are also likely to be using both crystallized and fluid intelligence to influence the actions we choose and the ways that choose to play them. What we are aiming for in this stage is to embed the learning to such a degree that we do not need any effort to retrieve it once we are in the final, performance stage.

Stage three: Performance or 'flow'

In stage three is the point at which we have learned, and we can work without effort. We focus on engaging with everything that happens in our environment, and *we want to remain entirely in task-positive thought mode* for extended periods of time, which allows us to be in a state of focused concentration, which keeps self-related thought at bay. We want to change the world and the people we see around us, and we want to have the freedom to focus entirely on that. We are still learning, but only in terms of what is happening in the immediate environment – we are catching new clues/ideas in terms of how everyone around moves and engages and attempts to change us, meaning that we are using both crystallized and fluid intelligence. We want to watch and react, but at this point in the work we want to keep our focus on our imagined world, looking for new clues and tactics that challenge our objectives, and we want to be open to responding to anything we did not expect. We are 'reading' the atmosphere, analysing facial expressions, physical movements, body language and any other signs that will help us understand the minds and the desires of the characters around us. We can only do all of this if we feel confident in everything we did in the first two stages, so that remembering text, movement and desired outcomes all feel automatic.

SUMMARY

1. Self-related thought does several damaging things to an acting performance, particularly when it takes the form of thinking about our bodies, past rehearsals, the way we said a line before, worrying about being judged or worrying about an audience response. But the biggest problem for an actor is that it sends us back into the past and into our own interior space and knocks us out of the present.

2. We need to consider and understand two modes of brain activity: default (creative, self-aware, non-attentional and wandering thought) and task-positive. Default mode spans time, and is useful in preparation stages, but task-positive thought remains in the present and it is where we want to be and what we want to employ when we are performing.

3. We also want to consider the different kinds of thinking that we bring to various stages of the work: convergent, divergent, lateral, crystallized and fluid intelligence.

4. We cannot control our thoughts by *trying* to control our thoughts. Instead, we can divert self-aware thought if we can focus our attention on a consuming task in the present.

5. We cannot take preparation thought into performance without compromising the quality and the experience of that performance.

6. The optimal mind state for performance is 'flow' state, and that may be related to mindfulness in the approach (we will be looking at this closely later in the book).

Memory

Part One: How memory works

Learning a text is where all actors begin. But few young actors begin that learning process in the right way – because few teachers seem to think that the way we learn a text is important. I believe that it is crucial. This follows on from my belief that the aim of most actors is to work in a way that allows them to focus externally on the imagined world around them. And the only way to do that is if text retrieval requires no effort. If text retrieval makes no demand on our (limited) cognitive resources during performance, it means that there is space freed up to allow us greater concentration on our imaginative connection with a scene, a partner, an objective. This chapter will focus on how we can work *with* memory to make our acting performances more secure and more pleasurable.

How did you ever learn all those lines?

Human memory is a complex and extraordinary thing, but most of us know little about just how it works beyond, perhaps, having a rough idea of the difference between long- and short-term memory. I think it is important that actors know more than this about how memory works, because the skill of building robust memory is the bedrock of the actor's work. I find it surprising that most acting books never talk about memory in terms of how, in the ordinary course of our craft, we are able to memorize great chunks of text verbatim. Instead, in most acting book indexes you will find memory associated with 'affective memory' or 'emotion memory'. I never took a single acting class (and I have taken many!) where the teacher spent even a moment talking to the class about something as fundamental as how we should set about memorizing text. It was expected, of course, and it seemed understood that we all had our own ways of memorizing text. Rehearsals often started with directors giving us an 'off-book' date. I know of educational and professional directors who insist that actors are off-book before the first rehearsal. If these directors understood a bit more about how memory works, they would never so consciously hinder their actors by laying down this requirement.

So as fundamental as it seems, I think it's important to talk about memory – not only of text, but of movement, environment and of what we are thinking and feeling when we're acting.

Types of memory

If you run a google check for 'types of memory' you will find many possibilities:

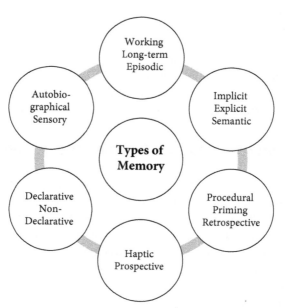

Confused? Don't worry – although there are certainly a lot of different types of memory to consider if you're a neuroscientist specializing in memory, as an actor all you have to be concerned with are three categories of memory: sensory, short-term (or working) and long-term. Long-term memory lasts and is more complex, so it has a lot of subsets, which is why you see so many listed above.

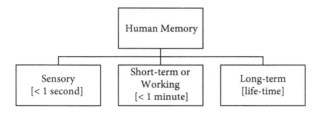

Long-term memory works in different ways, depending on just what it is that is being remembered.

As you can see, sensory memories (everything your senses are taking in right at this moment) last less than a second. Short-term, or working, memory lasts less than 1 minute. Because they're so brief, we don't have a lot of subsets underneath these two categories of memory, but we do have a lot of subsets under long-term memory.

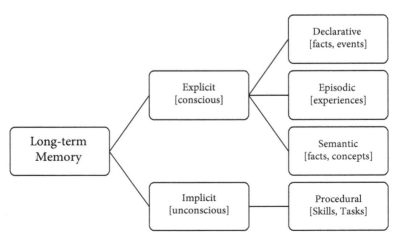

There are a lot of subsets to long-term memory because different kinds of skills and experiences are embedded through different pathways and places in the brain. As actors, we need to understand four types of memory:

- the kind of memory that we use in a short-term way;

- the kind of memory that stays with us for a long time;

- the kind of memory we are conscious of;

- the kind of memory we are not conscious of.

Most people know that there is a difference between long- and short-term memory. Depending on who or what you read, you can find different terms for short-term memory and this is because short-term memory does a variety of things. You are conscious of one of these right now. You are reading this book and this sentence (in an environment that might have other things to draw your attention), and to make sense of this sentence, you're having to hold the first part of the sentence in your head right the way through until you get to the end of the sentence. Now that is a long and confusingly structured sentence, but you probably got it! That is because your short-term memory can hold onto enough language to see you through to the end of even a badly constructed sentence (provided you can maintain your attention). Short-term memory is often called 'working memory' – it works to hold things for a short time (1–20 seconds), after which decisions must be made about what you want to hold onto and what you think you can let go. That is the whole purpose of working memory. There are a lot of mysteries still about working memory – not the least of which is how attention operates in working memory. But let's make this easier by thinking about how things happen in practice.

Let us suppose that along with my morning cup of coffee I am reading a good book. This requires that I use my working memory to make sense of the language and the sentence structure in the book. But while I am doing this, I might be aware of the nagging feeling that I must stop reading and get ready for work. Where did this nagging feeling come from? It might be any number of things:

1. I knew roughly what time it was when I started reading and roughly how long I've been reading (an internal cue).

2. I am aware that it's getting lighter outside (an external cue).

3. I hear the news on the radio, reminding me that it's 8.00 am (an external cue).

4. My legs are going numb from being crossed (an internal cue).

What we know from looking at this list is that while my short-term working memory is focused on my book, other parts of my brain are beavering away – hearing things, feeling things, remembering things. I might choose to pay attention to these things, or I might choose not to pay attention to these things. But rumbling along underneath all of them are a couple of long-term memories: what time I routinely start getting ready on a work day, what getting ready for a work day entails, what time I have to be at work and how long it will take me to get to work.

What working memory does is take in information. It can't hold that information for very long, however, unless we take those bits of information to the next stage: we can decide to keep paying attention to them in our working memory so that they stay with us. The information we take in with working memory might be an external sensory one – a sound, a colour, a brightening morning light. Or it might be internal – a 'feeling' that time is going by, a sensation that my legs are getting numb. Different kinds of information use different parts of the working memory. But for our purposes, we need only be aware that working memory is the thing that allows us to communicate with and make sense of our immediate environment. The important thing to note in this small example is that at any given moment there are a lot of things going on in our minds, and a lot of quick – sometimes unconscious – memories being 'played' and decisions being made. This morning I decided to keep paying attention to what I was reading, and I decided to put off getting up to get ready for work. But in making those decisions I was aware of many things being held briefly in my working memory.

Processes of memory

Along with thinking about the kind of memory we are conscious of, we need to think also about three stages of conscious memory: sensing, encoding and retrieving:

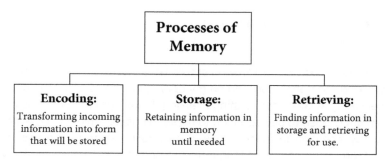

For an actor, how do these stages work in practice?

Let's imagine we are attending a first read-through of a script. If you are a well-prepared actor, you will have read the script on your own before the read-through, so you aren't encountering the words or the story for the first time. But it is likely that you are encountering a lot of other ideas for the first time. For example, you might be surprised at the way another actor interprets something, or surprised at your own responses, or at the way the director envisions a particular scene. In this situation, you are sensing a lot of new things. You will be making some decisions about which of the many new things you are encountering need to be remembered. Some things are simple and don't need much work to encode.

Let us imagine that the director tells you he wants you to do the part with a French accent. This might surprise you, but if you have a natural facility with dialects and have done a French accent before, this will simply mean relying on your long-term memory to apply knowledge of the right technical choices in creating this accent and applying it to this text. But perhaps the director also tells you that he wants you to master some popular social dances of the early nineteenth century for the role. And while it will not be hard to remember the direction, the task itself will take some work. Not only because you aren't likely to be able to reel off a list of popular social dances of the early nineteenth century (are you?!) but this also means that along with your research, you will need some practice in order to gain the kind of motor skills that will allow you to do the dances as if you've been doing them for many years.

So, off you go to learn about the dances and the first stage is research. Once you have gathered enough information about the sequences of the dances, in rehearsal you will need to remember and apply that information. This will require some physical work on the dance steps and sequences that you can rehearse and then remember for use later. This means that you used your working memory to access the information about popular social dancing in the early nineteenth century, and you managed to *encode* some of that information (you stored it away in your long-term memory). Then you *retrieved* some of that information (managed to find it and bring it to your conscious mind) for use in rehearsal. The history of dance and the way that people engaged with dance at social gatherings may be part of what you have encoded and will want to apply or discuss in rehearsal. But you will only be able to apply and use the dance in rehearsal if you have spent time learning the physical movements involved in the dance.

As we know, when we first learn a physical skill, it takes some thinking about. But as we practise more and more, the movements begin to feel as if they are happening effortlessly and without thought. When movement begins to feel 'automatic' it means that you have transferred the sequence of the dance steps from your working to your long-term memory. Once you get into rehearsal and have time to repeat the sequences you will ultimately be able to do the dance without thinking about it. In the process of your rehearsals, you will have been using your procedural memory to call upon the learned skill of using a French accent and the learned skill of performing a nineteenth-century social dance.

But we still have all that text to learn. And at this point we need to think more closely about how memory works. Because we can either set all the right conditions for learning that text, or we can set all the wrong ones.

Text and memory

As we have seen, long-term memory is different from short-term memory as it has the capacity to retain things over a much longer time and the retrieval can sometimes feel effortless. This varies in many ways, of course. Some people seem able to encode and retrieve memories in a most extraordinary way. Some people can read a book once and retain an extraordinary amount of detail from that single reading – even many years after the reading. I, on the other hand, must work much harder to retain that kind of detail and often – even with that effort – will struggle to retain detail after reading. Some people find the work of encoding challenging, and this can often depend on what it is we are trying to encode. For example, I find anything mathematical hard to encode. But some people have a harder time retrieving, and all of us have known that sensation from time to time of not being able to retrieve something that we KNOW we know. So, what is it that we are doing when we are encoding and retrieving things and what do actors need to know about the process?

Probably first and foremost, we need to understand that memory as a whole is very complex and never as straightforward as we think. Memory retrieval is also a complex thing – but it is important for actors to know that encoding and retrieval are highly interlinked. *In other words, how we learn and store is deeply connected to how we retrieve.*

Most actors know instinctively (or have learned by experience) that memory retrieval is 'context-dependent'. That sounds complicated, but all it means is that we retrieve memories in a way that is connected to what was going on during the *storing* of the memory. How do you know this? Watch what happens when an actor – who knows their line perfectly when pouring a cup of tea during a scene – is suddenly told that the staging is going to change, and the teapot and the sofa will be cut. The actor will go back to the same spot in rehearsal and for the first few times almost invariably they will forget the text that went with pouring the tea. Of course, after a few times, the new line will be learned in a new context and all will be fine. But changing physical cues means that part of the retrieval cue is gone and therefore it's harder to bring the line to mind. This is because, without knowing it, the actor learned both the action and the line at the same time.

It is also helpful for actors to know that there are two important kinds of retrieval. One is *associative retrieval*. This kind of retrieval means that the memory is associated with things. If I ask you right now to remember the word 'banana' you will almost certainly (involuntarily) find that certain things come to mind – it might be 'yellowness', a curved shaped or even perhaps the particular taste or texture of a banana. That's because you associate these sensations with your experience of bananas. This example demonstrates associative retrieval. The more associations you make ('yellowness', taste, texture, shape or how you slice them on your cereal), the more likely it is you will remember the word if I ask you what the word was at some point next week. But if I ask you to remember the word 'augend', unless you are that rare person who knows what the word means, you are far less likely to be able to remember the word when I ask you about it next week. This is because you may not be able to create quick associations that might help you remember. Consequently, when I ask you what the word was next week, unless you created specific associative links (for example 'augend' sounds sort of like 'oh-gend' and maybe in order to remember I decided to think of an agenda that would shock people who might then cry 'Oh'!) you are unlikely to recall the word. But if you did go to that extra 'Oh-gend'/agenda effort, the associated ideas would probably enable you to recall the word.

When memory requires a bit of work, it has a different name: it's called *effortful or strategic retrieval*.

Memory expert Daniel Schacter explains: 'Associative retrieval occurs when a cue automatically triggers an experience of remembering. Everyone is familiar with this sort of experience: hearing a favorite song reminds you of where you were when you first heard it ... The other retrieval process, which is referred to as effortful or strategic retrieval, involves a slow, deliberate search of memory ... '[1]

He also points out that these types of memory are not only different, but that they use different parts of the brain. Associative retrieval relies on the hippocampus and other medial temporal lobe

---

[1] Schacter (1996): 68.

structures. These parts of the brain are not involved in your 'central control' or executive thinking; they work automatically in this kind of retrieval which is why it feels as if it is easy for you. The effortful or strategic retrieval works through the regions of the prefrontal cortex – the area you use to do your planning, thinking and communicating. That makes sense, since in the effortful retrieval you are having to think in order to retrieve memory.

Clearly, when we're performing a scene, we're hoping that we will be able to draw on our *associative retrieval*, because it is effortless. But of course, sometimes the lines just go, and we're forced to do an effortful or strategic retrieval (the 'slow deliberate search') in the attempt to get it back again. So how do we ensure that we are always using associative retrieval? To begin with, we need to be sure that we are encoding text memory in the best possible way.

Effective encoding

Understanding the way memories are encoded is extremely complex and best left to neuroscientists, but the important thing for actors to note is that encoding is a kind of holistic thing. It takes *everything* into account. Think of it this way: when you take a photograph of your cat doing something cute, you're trying to get the best picture of your cat's cuteness that you can. But the final product is a picture that includes everything in the environment: the mess in the living room behind cute cat, the snippet of your dog's tail that is also in the picture, the edge of your thumb, which was slightly in view of the lens on your smart phone, and the framed photo of your last holiday that is on the side table. Now of course, you're just thinking that this is a cute picture of your cat, and that is probably where your attention remains. Nevertheless – *the rest of the context stays in the picture*. And that is just how your memory works.

In a famous experiment, two groups of people were asked to recall a list of common words. Group A was simply given the list of words and then asked a week later to recall them. Overall, they did well. Group B, however, was first asked to smoke a little marijuana. Once they had done this, they (like Group A) were given a list of words to remember. When Group B came back a week later and were asked to recall the words in a sober state they did quite poorly. But once they smoked a little marijuana again, their scores improved! This well-known experiment was run with other substances – alcohol and various stimulants – and always it was found that *people remember best when they are in the same state that they were in at the time of encoding a memory.* This is called state-dependent retrieval.

When you encode memory, a lot of things are included: what you were doing, where you were, what you were hearing, how you were feeling. Think about this for a moment. How do you usually learn your lines? Suppose you are cast in a production where the director has specified that you must arrive on the first day with all your lines learned. Perhaps, like so many actors, you spent hours sitting in your bedroom or living room, script in front of you, saying lines over and over again and slowly trying to cram them into your memory. If you had some cooperative friends, you may have been able to open a bottle of wine and invite them over to go through your lines with you so that you could hear the other lines being spoken. But of course, where and how you learned your lines will accompany your retrieval of the actual lines once you're in rehearsal. Consequently, you won't just remember: 'Yea, and I will weep a while longer'. You might also remember that you were lying on your bed and what you could see was the script and your bedroom ceiling. Or you might remember you and your friends feeling a bit squiffy, lying on the sofa, and giggling as you got to 'Yea, and I will weep a while longer' in your living room at 11.00 pm.

But once you arrive at your first rehearsal (where you find yourself in a bright warm studio, looking at a particularly handsome actor and feeling pretty alert and eager to make a good impression), you may well to find it tough to retrieve those lines from Act IV of *Much Ado About Nothing*. Not impossible, but it will be tougher going than if you were back in your bedroom looking at the ceiling, or in your living room after a few glasses of wine giggling with friends. Because the bright studio, the handsome actor, the different mood are all things that memory scientists would term 'interference'. In other words, this is all new stimulus, and that new stimulus is interfering with the holistic (bedroom/ceiling/wine/friends/living room) memory that you had originally encoded.

Memory and 'mood congruence'

But of course, memory is also 'state-dependent' in terms of emotion as well. And for actors, this is really important. We are going to look closely at emotion later and the question of just how 'real' an actor's emotion in performance is or can be. But the way an actor displays or feels an emotional state – however we might think of that emotional state (either 'real' or 'simulated') – is part of what gets encoded along with the overall memory of a text. Memory experts often call this 'mood congruency' and it means that we remember an emotion or feeling that we've encoded along with the text we've memorized. Every year, during audition season, I feel like I am running an experiment in memory and 'mood congruency' repeatedly and getting the same results.

If you've ever auditioned for drama school, you may have been asked to try your audition monologue in a different way. This is called a 're-direct' and every drama school I have worked at uses the re-direct in either first round or recall auditions. Re-directs are a quick way to test a candidate's flexibility and to see how they take direction. They are also useful if you think the candidate hasn't shown enough range in the material presented, and you want to see how they use (or if they *have*) more colours on their palette. So, for example, an auditionee might do two very intense, dark readings and someone behind the desk might ask for one of those pieces to be played very differently – in a lighter or less serious way.

Most actors are used to this kind of re-direct and know that a director is just looking for different qualities in their performance. And most actors – especially in an audition – are also happy to give the new direction a go. The problem is that once you've learned your Queen Margaret speech with the intention of making Henry feel ashamed of himself, you will quickly realize that along with the text you were learning your intention. And with intention comes the memory of what it felt like to play that particular action or intention. So when you are asked in a re-direct to play the speech as if you're trying to make Henry laugh, you will find it very hard to remember the text that you just recited so brilliantly while you were attempting to make Henry feel ashamed of himself. Changing the intention that you learned along with your text (and the emotional force that is naturally generated when playing that intention) now critically *interferes* with your ability to retrieve that same text.

I do a lot of re-directs in audition and I would say that at least 90 per cent of the actors that I re-direct find it impossible to retrieve text easily when playing a new intention. Clearly, we are learning much more than lines when we are learning lines! But what makes memory stick in the first place?

Elaborative encoding

Encoding memory in a way that really stays with us is often called elaborative encoding by brain scientists. Elaborative encoding is probably why people who do not act are astonished at how well actors can remember lines.

Often when I ask an actor how they learned their text I get four answers as standard:

1. I write down all the lines in a notebook.

2. I say the lines over and over again.

3. I record the lines and listen back to them.

4. I just keep reading them over and over again.

From what we have considered in the last few pages you should be able to see now why these methods are not ideal.

Elaborative encoding is a way of relating ideas or places to the things to be memorized, and there are some helpful ways in which we can do this.

A well-known experiment in elaborative encoding conducted in 1982 by researchers Bradshaw and Anderson asked to two study groups to recall a sentence:

'Mozart made a long journey from Munich to Paris.'

The first group was given only the sentence and were instructed to remember it. The second group was provided with some additional information related to the sentence, such as 'Mozart wanted to leave Munich to avoid a romantic entanglement,' or 'Mozart was intrigued by musical developments coming out of Paris'. The two additional sentences are providing information about what motivated Mozart to leave Munich and what motivated him to go to Paris. After a week, both groups returned and were asked to recall the sentence. The group given the information about what motivated Mozart's trip outperformed the group that was simply asked to recall the sentence with no other information.[2]

What is interesting about Bradshaw and Anderson's experiment is that it made clear how additional information – in this case about motivation – becomes part of a retrieval cue. And for us, it makes clear why the work of an actor (which involves much thought about what motivates the behaviour of a character) is an advanced version of elaborative encoding. The kind of memory that involves this kind of additional information is called semantic memory. It is the memory that we use when we're recalling what we know about things. In the Bradshaw and Anderson experiment the second group knew some information about why Mozart wanted to leave Munich and why he was interested in going to Paris. We could deepen that information (with imaginative visualization, etc.) and my guess is that doing so would make this sentence even easier to remember. But for now, it is enough for us to know that additional information about things like what motivated Mozart's trip makes it easier for us to remember that he made the trip.

This small example reminds us as well of why the work actors do in rehearsal and preparation is always deeply entwined in encoding text. Throughout the whole of our stage one preparation and stage

---

[2]Bradshaw and Anderson (1982).

two rehearsals, which includes all the text work we do on our own and all the rehearsals we do with a company, we want to enhance and strengthen that elaborative encoding process. We want to use elaborative encoding to make sure that our text memory works so well that when it comes to performance, we are relying simply on associative retrieval (which feels effortless) and not on effortful or strategic retrieval (which takes work). And in fact, we want to be at the point where the retrieval of lines isn't really an issue because the lines are so secure in memory that they feel 'automatic'.

The blissful state of 'automaticity'

Are there some lines in your head that you just 'know'? Most actors have some small bits of text in their heads that they seem to retain for some reason. Sometimes these are segments of monologues that you had or still have in your repertoire. Sometimes they are just parts of text that stayed with you even though you couldn't say why. Whatever the reason for these memories, the fact is they are there, and you don't have to work hard at retrieving them. They have passed into a kind of memory that is sometimes called 'automatic' or 'automaticity'. Like associative memory, they take no effort. For actors, *this is an ideal place to be*. Because (as we considered earlier) what we can hold in our conscious mental workspace (our 'cognitive load') at any one time is strictly limited. And that means we must be incredibly efficient in the use of that conscious mental working space.

Working WITH memory

As you might imagine, there have been some academic studies done on how actors memorize large amounts of text for performance. The best known of these are the studies carried out by Helga and Tony Noice, and I am always surprised at how few actors know of their research. The good news for actors is that their research has found that acting improves general cognitive performance and may even enhance cognitive performance long-term. Their studies have shown marked improvement in brain processing in adults, and they attribute this to the kinds of activities that go on in the 'acting brain'. The acting brain does much more than simply think because as we act, we are involving thinking, feeling and doing, which means that there is a kind of holistic interaction that seems to be strengthening the overall connections between the thinking, motor and emotion areas of the brain. That is clearly beneficial.

But the basis of most of their study has been in how it is that actors can remember so much verbatim dialogue.

Of course, when we first encounter a script, we are simply hoping to get the gist of what is going on. This is the way that a first reading of a play occurs – we follow the story along to get the general gist and to understand the arc of the narrative. Most people could read the first scene of Hamlet and tell you what happened: on a cold night a couple of men encounter a ghost. It looks to them like the late king and they decide that someone should tell the king's son. But of course, as they progress, actors must dig deeper to find out much more than the general gist of a scene.

We can demonstrate this with the first three lines:

Bernardo: Who's there?
Francisco: Nay, answer me: stand, and unfold yourself.
Bernardo: Long live the king!

There are only thirteen words here, but to an actor, so much is conveyed – first about environment: it is dark and foggy and these two soldiers – who clearly know each other – can't see who is speaking. Bernardo is coming to take over the watch from Francisco but cannot see him. Francisco, who is still on guard, knows that HE is the one who should be asking the questions, so he turns Bernardo's question back on him. He orders him to stand (meaning, I think, stay still) and 'unfold' himself. He doesn't say 'what's your name' because clearly, it's too soon for that. I think 'unfold' here means perhaps remove your hat so I can see your face or open your cloak so I can see what weapons you (may) have. Bernardo counters with 'long live the king' to make clear his allegiance and probably to make clear through voice and accent that he is a fellow countryman.

If you are just a reader of this text, you do not get much from it. But if you take it apart the way an actor must – as demonstrated above – you get an impressive amount of information from thirteen words. The detailed analysis required by the actor's preparation means that from the very first they are embellishing and encoding information.

In several experiments, the Noice studies confirmed that this kind of analysis is what aids an actor's surprising ability to remember so many lines perfectly. But beyond just the detail of what the language is conveying, they also found other components of the actor's process that are effective in terms of memory.

One of the Noice experiments used two groups, both of which were given a text that they were told to memorize. The participants in Group A were told simply to remember the text in any way that they could. The second group, Group B, were given the same text but they were told NOT to try to remember it. Instead, the members of Group B were asked to approach the text like an actor (they were asked to speak the text out loud, trying to 'mean what you say'). Surprisingly, Group B – the group asked NOT to try to remember their lines – invariably remembered the text better than Group A who were asked to try to memorize it.

This study concluded that the reasons for this were complex:

1. The 'acting' group (B) were doing what memory researchers would call 'extensive elaboration' – in other words, they were embellishing the words through imagination.

2. The 'acting' group were taking a perspective (by adopting the point of view of a character).

3. The 'acting' group were relating the thoughts and feelings of the character to their own thoughts and feelings.

4. The 'acting' group were using 'mood congruency' relating to the general emotional content of the script and sometimes reproducing it when they tried to say the words as if they meant them.[3]

---

[3]Noice and Noice (1997).

The same researchers also studied experienced actors and found that the tendency to break down scripts into units and to break lines down into determining the character's goals also greatly aided memory. What the Noices have proved, in fact, is that our usual work as actors does much of the memorization for us – but only when we are learning in context, with intent and physical action.

But so often, rather than trusting this process for memorization, actors attempt instead to do what Group A in the experiment related above did – they just try to learn the text in any rote way that they can. Let's go back to the most common answers I get when I ask young, training actors how they learn lines:

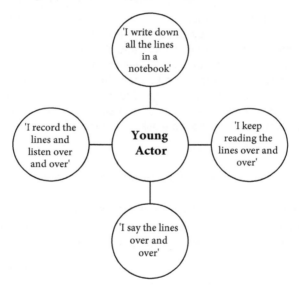

As I look at this, it seems clear to me what they are trying to do. In the first method, the actor is attempting to engage both physical (motor) skills and visual perception in memory. But of course, in this case, the motor skills being encoded (writing) have nothing to do with the motor skills that the actor is going to want to be using when physicalizing a scene in rehearsal or performance. This is bound to create 'interference' in the retrieval.

In the second method, the actor is attempting to engage visual memory. It seems to me that some actors are more visually oriented than others. If you're the kind of actor who can sometimes actually see the line on the page (including the page itself) while you're saying it, you may be a more visually oriented actor. But this visual memory can interfere with memory in rehearsal or performance because what you want to see in these practical working situations is the imagined world around you and not some text on a page.

In the third and fourth of these methods, the actor is attempting to make a 'phonological loop' stick in the long-term memory. Phonological loops are sounds we use often for quick memory. For example – put this book down and try to memorize this phone number quickly: 632 5407.

I am willing to bet that when you were trying to remember this number, you said or whispered the numbers repeatedly. This is what memory researchers call a 'phonological loop'. Sometimes you simply rehearse the numbers over and over silently, which is a kind of silent phonological loop. These loops decay quickly unless you carry on rehearsing them, and no actor wants to rehearse or perform by simply concentrating on saying a line quickly over and over again. In fact, all four of these methods tend to be ineffective in comparison with *simply doing what actors are meant to be doing*: paying extremely close attention to language, and character objectives. Researchers Helga and Tony Noice concluded that the reason actors seemed to have a superior ability to recall language accurately was that 'the actor attends closely to the exact wording of the script for the purpose of gaining clues to interpretation'.[4] You can see this clearly when you evaluate all the information we were able to glean from just three opening lines of *Hamlet*.

This means that actors help their memory process most when they are examining language closely and trying to understand why a character might use a specific word or phrase. They also enhance the encoding process by adopting a character's point of view and trying to 'mean what they are saying'.

Of course, when you are first learning lines you often do not know all the specific information you will eventually uncover through hours of rehearsal and discussion. *But that is entirely my point.* Trying to learn lines without the kind of depth and embellishment you discover in subsequent rehearsal is a large part of what creates the mental

---

[4]Two approaches to learning (Noice 1996).

battle that I so often see in young actors. It is not surprising that the Noice research so often concentrates on actors with ten or more years of experience – this is because experienced actors have generally learned the importance of applying the detail they have discovered in rehearsal when learning a text.

The overall lesson of this chapter is that we cannot set ourselves 'off-book' dates. For all that this is common practice, it works against our ability to learn text in the very best way possible. 'Off-book' dates force us into the worst kind of memorization techniques – rote drilling, phonological looping, etc. – and these techniques inspire effort*ful* rather than effort*less* retrieval. In preparation and rehearsal, as we do a close, careful analysis of text, we generally find that the text is encoding into our brains as we're rehearsing. Working with an ensemble or partner and moving while speaking is an important part of the learning and will also help to encode text as we rehearse. Wherever we can't remember, we can usually go back a see what it is that hasn't been thought through carefully enough (Why does this idea occur to the character right at this moment? Why these particular words?) Once we know why these particular words or ideas are important this generally provides the context that triggers effortless retrieval.

SUMMARY

1. There are different types of memory, and actors need to know how each works so that they can understand the process that helps us to transfer things from our short-term working memory into our long-term memory.

2. Memory occurs in three stages: encoding, storage, retrieval, and there are two types of retrieval for us to consider – associative retrieval (which feels effortless) and effortful or strategic retrieval (which requires conscious work). We always want to aim for effortless retrieval when performing, so the work we do in stages one and two is critical.

3. Never attempt to learn lines too soon or in a 'rote' way. If you do, you will be working against the natural process of embellishment and elaboration that the acting process

requires, and which are of critical importance in building effortless retrieval.

4. Memory is context-dependent, which means that when you learn lines, you are learning much more than just the text. Make sure that when you're learning lines, you're doing so as often as you can in rehearsal, with the right movement, intention and 'emotional force' or 'mood-congruence'.

5. We should not set 'off-book' dates for ourselves – instead we need to keep elaborating and encoding text through rehearsal and analysis until retrieval feels effortless.

Part Two: How do I use this knowledge in practice?

As we know, the optimal memory condition in performance is effortless retrieval. In that optimal state we will not even be thinking about memory in performance, because retrieval will feel automatic. If we are not at that effortless retrieval stage, we are not ready to perform. Most actors have lost lines often enough in rehearsal to know that spending effort trying to retrieve a line takes you right out of the moment and radically interferes with your ability to engage in an imagined world around them.

But we can still find important ways to support our memory in the preparation and rehearsal stages.

Stage One: Preparation

Take time to explore the ways in which you 'unit' or break scenes down into segments while learning

Units are a very important weapon in an actor's arsenal. Careful and thoughtful uniting does much to help encode text and aid retrieval, so how we do this really matters. But it is a slightly controversial area. Some people worry about too many units, which might make an actor feel that the text they are learning becomes too fragmented.[5] But research has shown that the way actors unit can have great benefit in terms of how we retrieve text.

As you may have suspected, Helga and Tony Noice did some research[6] into this area and discovered that when actors break a text down into different thought units and then linked these units to goal-directed activity, the result was far higher rates of effortless retrieval. They found that actors demonstrated 50 per cent superior recall from the non-actor group because they were trained to create text units and to describe each unit from a character's perspective and goals.

The Noice research also found that even though each actor was looking at the same text, they often came up with different unit 'break' points and different goal descriptions. I think this underlines the fact that the way in which we break a text down into units is a subjective thing.

I think there are two ways we can use this research in our own practice. The first is that careful and detailed uniting of a text in the early phase is of significant help in the encoding and retrieval of that text. The second is that in terms of text memorization, it does not seem to matter if the units or the description of those units is 'right' – only that it is done in a way that makes sense to the actor.

This means that in stage one of learning, you want to break the text down into units that feel right to you (remember, there is no 'right or wrong' here – just what makes sense to you) and that you do this from the point of view of your character. I think it is most helpful to do this in terms of where you feel the character thought is changing. But it is clear that even at this early stage, you want to be thinking about what the ideal outcome for the character you are playing would be. That gives you a basis for thinking about 'goal-directed' activity.

---

[5]Consider this section from Bella Merlin's excellent *The Complete Stanislavsky Toolkit*: 'in the early stages of breaking down a scene into its composite BITS, it's not very helpful to have too many divisions ... try not to over-fragment the text' (2014: 72).
[6]Noice and Noice (1993).

Rethink how – and with whom! – you learn

If this chapter has taught you anything, I hope it is that *what we do in performance is going to be massively affected by how we learn and how we memorize.* The great majority of the learning that I see most actors do centres on the analysis of text – breaking into units, planning out actions, analysing character – which generally involves the actor thinking on their own about a character in a situation. In other words, the work seems to progress like this:

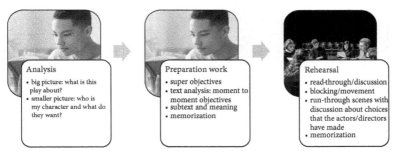

First and second image credits: Shutterstock; third image courtesy of Edinburgh Napier University.

If you look at this process, you see that it illustrates something fairly common: that we tend to do a lot of our thinking, preparation and memorization in isolation. This, in turn, suggests that much of our work can be done by thinking things through by ourselves. We seem to see acting as an intellectual labour in the early stages: we make discoveries about a piece by analysing, considering our choices and then making our choices. We consider what the circumstances are, what we say and do in those given circumstances and what other characters say about us in the text. We put these things together and make some 'executive' choices about what we are going to do once we get into rehearsal.

But I see some changes on the horizon in terms of this kind of process and I think those changes are helpful. Practitioners like Tina Landau and Anne Bogart introduced 'Viewpoints' training into the American theatre scene over the last two decades, and increasingly this more ensemble-based working pattern has become a regular part of training in the US. Much of the work is about movement in space, reacting to other people, to proximity, to gesture and movement. In effect, Viewpoints reverses the process outlined above and looks a bit more like this:

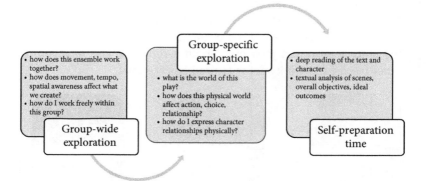

In Viewpoints, a much greater majority of preparation time is spent with a company, even at an early stage. Early decisions are made while actors are surrounded by environment, perception and action. Contemporary research reveals that:

- Thought and action are deeply intertwined.

- Thought and action are constantly in communication with each other.

- Thought and action are continually surrounded by and adapting to environment and making decisions about action.

This means that if we want to simulate human intelligence in an organic way as actors, we must be more conscious of the importance of environment, action and response when we're planning, memorizing and carrying out our work as actors. This in turn means that even in the very early stages of our work, we should try not to work too often in isolation, because much of the learning and memory work we need to do has to be generated by responding to environment. If we attempt a lot of isolated intellectual work, we miss the opportunity not only to learn from an ensemble experience (even if that ensemble is only you and one other person), but we also miss the opportunity to be a crucial part of building a shared sense of the imagined world we are going to be inhabiting together.

It might help to think about the ways in which human beings create a field of energy that flows between them in communication. We rarely speak of this energy, but we feel it all the time. We often find other peoples' energy contagious, and we can tell when either positive or negative energy is flowing between the members of a group. Acting is a dynamic, fluid process that passes along on the currents of this energy, and not a 'single agent' process. This means that working with a group early in our work allows us to feel our part in that process and makes each actor more receptive and aware of the way that the group creates and shares energy.

Within that shared group energy, try to remember that by focusing on sending your energy outward, you make a significant impact. You have the power to use your creative energy and ideas to make the other actors in the group better. By giving the other actors greater and more challenging stimuli they will, in response, give you opportunities to respond more deeply and more energetically. It is the flow of this energy in stimulus and response that makes the group experience so powerful in suppressing or diverting self-conscious thought. Here lies the zen of acting: by focusing on making all the actors around you better, you make yourself a better actor.

Get your body involved even at the earliest stages

Research has consistently shown that movement significantly increases and extends brain power. When you are researching or reading, include movement in your exploration right from the start. As you are reading about that nineteenth-century Russian society, imagine 'moving through it' in the dress and company of the day. Find imaginative dream scenarios you can move through in a playful exploratory way. If you are playing Francisco, walk the battlements of the castle in the fog, feeling the cold and the weight of the uniform, coat and weapons. Imagine listening as you walk for any sound or movement that might mean the ghost is nearby. Choose particular lines that fascinate you and 'move through' them. The brain understands abstract concepts best by casting them in metaphorical physical terms. Thus, we may be, as Francisco, 'petrified', or 'jumpy' or as if 'my heart is in my mouth'. Embodying abstract concepts in a physical way not only enhances memory but it also helps you connect physically with text in a meaningful way and may prevent rehearsal movement from interfering with text memory.

Stage Two: Rehearsal and experimentation

Be specific and elaborate with text in your rehearsals

Rehearsal is the place to learn lines, and that means we need to be analysing, always, why a character uses the specific words they use. This is partly because that specificity really aids secure memorization, but it is also because there are so many clues in language when we force ourselves to read in a specific and never in a general way.

One of the great joys of rehearsal is in trying to puzzle out why a character uses specific words or phrases. For example: it isn't enough to decide that when Hamlet says:

Oh that this too, too solid flesh would melt

that he means that he wishes he could disappear. If he meant that he wished he could disappear, he would probably say:

Oh How I wish I could disappear

But instead of dreaming about disappearing, he talks about flesh. He has chosen to think about flesh melting. This is an incredibly evocative description of what he wants right at that moment, and the minute he thinks about flesh he probably thinks about his mother and her flesh, and her sexual relationship with his uncle – both of whom he has just seen. Both of whom have probably reminded him that human, fleshly passions can be as disgusting as they can be exciting. When you are aware of all that, you are probably going to do something exciting/interesting with this line and not 'translate' it into something dull like 'I wish I could disappear'.

It is always a gift to an actor to encounter language that is unlike our own, because it helps to slow us down and think hard about why the word makes sense to this character in this situation. And the very act of thinking that through is a big part of encoding the word into memory.

In one research project an actor was asked about a line said by the character of the Mayor, from Ben Hecht's *The Front Page*: 'Don't pester me now, please'.[7] This is a short line and probably would not challenge us to remember even out of context. Still, actors generally have a lot of text to remember and sometimes short rather general lines like this can challenge our ability to remember them verbatim. Unless, of course, we think deeply about them.

The actor in this particular research project explained three things about his analysis in the early stages of learning: 1) the character uses the word 'pester', which he felt was the kind of language we generally use to describe children's behaviour, therefore he felt it was likely that the Mayor saw the person he was speaking to as childish, or at least inferior to him in power; 2) the alliterative use of 'pester' and 'please' suggested that the Mayor's ego might be proud of his ability to employ an alliterative phrase; and 3) the Mayor is talking to a reporter who might be useful in the future, so the addition of the word 'please' keeps the door open for future encounters.

As you read through this actor's thought process you can almost certainly understand why being so careful and specific with language is an important part of both preparation and rehearsal phases for an actor. Tempting though it might be (and given how often I see actors do it!) to rush along and just play an action or an emotion in the early phases of the work, I hope to persuade you that the reward for paying extremely close attention to language from the start is not only a greater security of memory, but it also means that the language becomes much more muscular – and that means it becomes a much more powerful weapon in your work.

---

[7]Noice and Noice (2006).

Rehearse physically without text

Try playing whole scenes without text. Too often language dominates what we do and we don't give ourselves the chance to connect with our bodies easily. Try a scene without dialogue but keep thoughts and intentions. Allow the way you explore and inhabit a space to do the work that the language usually does for you. Notice what changes when language is not driving all of the actions.

Make the space your 'home'

Really explore the way that this set room affects you. How do the cold stone floor, rugs and open fires influence Macbeth's life and how does it affect his desires and his proximity to Lady Macbeth? Where is he most comfortable? Where can he relax? People discover that their personas are reflected back to them in spaces or objects. Does he have a chair that he imagines is a throne? Or do his chairs feel NOT throne-like, and therefore spur his ambition? Create relationships with *everything* around you. Do not wait until the last week to work with the right props – get them into rehearsal as soon as you possibly can. It may be that the crude rim of her glass or mug tears at Lady Macbeth's heart and reminds her that she isn't living her best life. Giving life and meaning to objects around you helps to anchor your imagination in the world of the play.

Allow this phase to diagnose your preparation

There is always a phase in rehearsal when actors are attempting to work off-book and test their text retrieval. This is an important part of the learning, and it should never be rushed. It is always better to take more time to encode text securely than to rush the retrieval, as rushing can result in effortful retrieval, and we want to avoid that kind of effort when performing. This phase – where we can remember quite a lot of text, but not all of it, or where we remember the gist of text, but cannot retrieve and speak verbatim – is always a point to pay attention to in rehearsal.

You may recall that we talked about getting the gist of a text when we first read through material that is new to us. But when we are preparing, we start the process of elaborating (as we did above with the line 'Don't pester me now, please'). While I was writing this paragraph, I remembered the line as 'Don't pester me, please' – forgetting entirely about the word 'now'. So I got the gist of the line but not the line as written. That omission means that 'now' was the word I had not thought closely enough about. We had considered 'pester', 'please' and alliteration above. But not the word 'now'. With greater knowledge of this play I would know why this moment – now – is one during which the Mayor can't put up with any questions or pestering reporters. Is something urgent about to happen, or something urgent going on NOW? I must think with this kind of specificity if I want to make sure that I am able to recall text verbatim rather than generally.

The great thing about losing words or even lines in rehearsal, is that these points always diagnose your preparation well and pinpoint just where you need more work on encoding. Where you cannot recall is exactly where you need to dig deeper into that text. I am confident that if I have to recall the Mayor's line tomorrow or even next week, I won't forget the word 'now' because I've made the decision that I can't risk talking to reporters just as this moment because something urgent is happening.

You may also have had the experience where you feel you go 'dry' at the same point every time you rehearse a scene. I have watched this often as a director. Again, this is a good place to use that 'blank' mind moment to diagnose the preparation of text. This seems to happen much more often when I watch actors working on a monologue than it does when I watch actors working on a scene. I am guessing that this is because there are so many retrieval cues going on when you are working with a lot of actors around you. When you are working alone on something like an audition monologue, everything is up to you: imagining the world around you, imagining what the person you are speaking to is doing and imagining how things are changing around you as you speak. All that muscular imagination requires a lot of cognitive space. But when you find yourself going 'blank' in a monologue, or finding the monologue difficult to retain, it means you need to ask yourself more questions about the text. Sometimes it can be helpful to try editing a text.

For example, I worked with an actor who was struggling with Portia's speech on mercy from Act IV, scene I of *The Merchant of Venice*:

> The quality of mercy is not strained.
> It droppeth as the gentle rain from heaven
> Upon the place beneath. It is twice blessed:
> It blesseth him that gives and him that takes.
> 'Tis mightiest in the mightiest. It becomes
> The thronèd monarch better than his crown.
> His sceptre shows the force of temporal power,
> The attribute to awe and majesty
> Wherein doth sit the dread and fear of kings,
> But mercy is above this sceptred sway.
> It is enthronèd in the hearts of kings.
> It is an attribute to God himself.

The actor felt that the speech was repetitive, which she said made it hard to learn. I began by asking her to explain where the repetition was, and to help her preparation I suggested that she cut out anything that she found repetitive. As we went through the piece, she began to change her mind.

Initially she felt we could cut 'upon the place beneath', but then realized that the speech was very much about the way that heavenly mercy can/should be exercised on earth, so decided that this phrase needed to stay. She then thought that we did not need to talk about both the monarch's crown and the monarch's sceptre, but then realized that while the crown is that thing with which we most instantly identify kings, the sceptre is a symbol of kingly power and authority, so she decided that both needed to stay.

Her next thought was that 'Wherein doth sit the dread and fear of kings' could be cut, until we thought further about why the line was there. The line tells us that people both fear and dread a king's decision, but the rest of the speech moves from this fear and dread to something else: it explains how mercy combats this fear and dread and is therefore greater than earthly power: it is greater because it makes earthly power reflect God's mercy.

By the time we finished looking closely at what could be cut, or what was repetitive, we realized that the speech had NO repetition and that there was little or nothing to cut. The memorization of the text became easier. Often, and particularly with Shakespeare, text memory becomes much easier when we have looked this closely at meaning. And this means that trying to edit a text – even when you know that you can't or won't edit it for performance – is a good learning tool.

Getting past that 'mental block'

Sometimes actors hit what they identify as a 'mental block' against retrieving a particular part of dialogue. When this happens, you can always use the moment to think harder about why a character says this particular thing at this particular moment.

One way of confronting that 'dry' moment is to go back and make conscious links between a character's thought from one point to another. This will almost always undo the 'mental block'. Often, it is just at the point where character dialogue seems to veer off topic that we struggle to remember a line. This is a good example from Noel Coward's *Hay Fever*:

Sorel: I should like to be a fresh, open-air girl with a passion for games.
Simon: Thank God you're not.
Sorel: It would be so soothing.
Simon: Not in this house.
Sorel: Where's mother?

In this opening page of the play, Sorel and her brother are discussing her desire to be a different kind of person, then quickly jumps to a question about where their mother is. This kind of apparently non sequitur line is typical of the kind of moment where actors can struggle to remember what comes next. But if you look closely at this exchange, you realize that when Simon says the word 'house', the first thing that occurs to Sorel is their mother. This is because the house, its contents and the decisions made within it are all largely Judith's (their mother). Clearly, she is such an outsized character that the house symbolizes her in Sorel's head. Spending a little time to think about why 'house' makes 'mother' spring into Sorel's mind will almost certainly make the actor's retrieval of this line effortless.

Another way to make a longer piece of dialogue stick is to create a vivid memory as context for it. For example, Benedick has a lengthy description of Claudio's foolish behaviour after he has fallen in love:

> I have known when there was no music with him but the
> drum and the fife, and now had he rather hear the tabor and
> the pipe. I have known when he would have walked ten mile
> afoot to see a good armour, and now will he lie ten nights
> awake carving the fashion of a new doublet. He was wont
> to speak plain and to the purpose, like an honest man and a
> soldier, and now is he turned orthography; his words are a very
> fantastical banquet,
> just so many strange dishes.

The actor playing Benedick could create the memory of an afternoon when he and Claudio saw an army marching to drum and fife, and then decided to go buy Claudio an expensive new set of armour. This would help much in terms of creating a memory that inspires the very specific things that Benedick is complaining about here, and even the order in which he complains about them. He could go further and remember how blunt Claudio was when they were looking for the new set of armour, which might remind him of how 'plain and to the purpose' Claudio used to be when he did not like something.

But, importantly, don't just dream about this memory. Move it around. Move through it, as you watch the army parading in the street before you – follow them for a bit. Then move with Claudio down the street to where the armour smith's workshop might be and go into the workshop physically. Point toward different sets of armour. Perhaps try on a helmet and perhaps make a gesture toward Claudio to be quiet when you see he is being too blunt (too 'plain and to the purpose') about the armour he did not like in front of the armourer. The more you can move your body while you create this memory, the more powerful your recall will be. Research has repeatedly shown that when we embody what we want to learn, we learn more deeply and more securely.

Creating memories to inspire text and then moving through them physically is a great way to elaborate on what you are learning and gives you greater encoding power.

Get your body involved in physically demanding scenes as soon as possible

Actors generally hate holding scripts while they rehearse, but it is a necessary evil when we are just starting out in rehearsal and certainly better than confining the process to rote learning. Rehearsal is always the right place for learning lines and being patient with the process is key to moving text securely into a state where you can retrieve it without effort.

Sometimes, when working on a scene that is not particularly physical, holding a script and paying attention to the text as you work, watch and move does not create much difficulty. But when a scene IS highly physical, you need to recruit some help in the early rehearsals.

Trying to learn complex movement alongside text is a real challenge. In these instances, you will always do best by involving other actors. Start by giving your script to someone who can read your lines in while you are doing the movement. Focus on movement and listening for the first few attempts. Then slowly, as you repeat the work, start to speak along with the actor reading your lines whenever you find you can recall the language.

For example, I recently worked on a scene that involved two actors trying to hide a dead body when another character showed up unexpectedly. The process was demanding and very complex. As the actors explored all the physical possibilities of trying to hide a dead body in clever ways that would not alert the visitor, we had two other actors read their lines in from the side. Slowly, as we repeated the scene, the actors involved grew used to the movements and began speaking lines as they were read by the off-stage actors. By the time we had gone through the scene for an hour, the actors were pretty good at doing both lines and movement without help. This is because movement actually enhances the encoding process and makes the text easier both to learn and retain.

If we had tried to learn this scene in the usual way (actors learning lines first), we would have to have learnt it twice – once to lay the text down in memory, and then once to learn how to retrieve the text while executing complex movement. It saves time and makes the memorization much easier if you do both at once.

Character

Part One: How character works

Thinking about character

An actor's work often begins with the attempt to understand what drives behaviour. Sometimes we come at this question by using psychology. A theory like Freud's is based on the notion that we can understand some of our behaviour by uncovering trauma from our past (sometimes in unconscious ways like a 'slip of the tongue' or a dream). It was Freud's idea that this hidden trauma might now influence our behaviour, and that by unpeeling the layers of our past we might be able to better understand the motivation behind what could otherwise seem to us like mysterious behaviour patterns or actions. Many of us have grown up alongside this notion, and when approaching a role, we might employ this idea like this:

> Hamlet's (or any human's) behaviour is the manifestation of some deep, possibly unconscious trauma/drives/desires, etc. It follows, then, that these deep, possibly unconscious traumas/drives/desires, etc. are connected to Hamlet's 'character' – THEY ARE PART OF WHAT MAKES HIM WHO HE IS.

When preparing to work on a play or a scene, actors are in the business of analysing what drives and creates various kinds of behaviours in the characters they play.

Often this starts with what we can observe and then we work our way backwards to understand what has motivated behaviour. In other words, we 'reverse engineer' – we start from the observables and work our way back into discovering the origins of what we can observe in any given behaviour. Much of this 'reverse engineering' takes place first on an intellectual level, and we involve inhabiting that behaviour at a later stage.

For example, when we first read the 'nunnery' scene from *Hamlet*, we probably note that Hamlet seems very cold and rather angry with Ophelia when he meets up with her in Act III. He denies that he ever gave her any gifts, tells her that she should have no children and that there should be no more marriages. At this point we attempt to analyse or 'reverse engineer' this observable state. What has caused this behaviour? And in that analysis, we may notice:

- He seems to know that he is being watched, and perhaps suspects that he is being watched now (and has already said as much to Rosencrantz and Guildenstern as he knows the King and Queen have sent them to spy on him).

- He seems to have little regard for Ophelia's father and may suspect him of spying as well (he asks Ophelia where her father is and she lies to him, saying that he is at home).

- He seems to be suspicious of everything and everyone and seems to have concluded that people are all dishonest, including the woman he loves.

- He has temporarily lost his faith in humanity and this causes him to direct anger toward Ophelia as she may be involved (she is!) in the lies and deception that have driven him to some extreme action.

Now we have observable behaviour: *anger, coldness toward the woman he loves.* **And we can take that observable behaviour apart to analyse the 'workings' that are driving the behaviour:** *he has reasons to be angry (he is being spied on); he has reasons to be cold to poor Ophelia (she's part of this spying conspiracy).*

This kind of analysis gives us motivation. It means we are not just angry at Ophelia for no reason – we have good reason to be angry. Having made up our mind that Ophelia is betraying me, and that she is part of a whole system of betrayals, I now know how to act toward her.

Of course, while this analysis covers Hamlet's behaviour, it does not tell us much about his character. That is because at this moment he is facing a situation that is utterly unprecedented in his life. Indeed, over five acts we watch a young man trying to cope with a series of situations he has never faced before.

The question, then, is this: does it help us in our preparation to understand anything about Hamlet's psychology or even his 'character'? My answer would be a firm no, and I will spend some time in this chapter explaining why.

Thinking metaphorically

Years ago, when I was writing a different book, I grew interested in the ways that both actors and those who write about acting think about or conceptualize 'character'. I noticed that most of the time, when people talk about character, they tend to conceive the process of an actor's work on character through some fascinating metaphors. Most of these metaphors describe the 'character' as something distinct or as something distant from us as actors.

One common metaphor suggests that we see a character as a container. We hear people talking about:

Getting into the character
Getting inside the character

Another metaphor seems to suggest that a character is in a different location, and we must search or travel to locate them:

The background should lead you to your character[1]
How do I get from a **Real I** to a **Dramatic I**?[2]
Finding the character

One metaphor seems to pose the character you are playing as something distinctly apart from you (as a friend/potential enemy/ picture or image):

As soon as you know your character, your character will give you attitudes …[3]

---

[1]Adler (1988: 72).
[2]Benedetti (1998: 4).
[3]Adler (1988: 72).

When I confront the character I'm going to play ...[4]
Let us say that the actor has visualized the character in his imagination[5]
And one seems to pose the character as an object or servant:
Thus we master the character ... We master his thoughts and feelings[6]
You must master your characterization[7]

All these metaphors pose a kind of 'split' between an actor and the character that they play. But how can it help us as actors to think in this way? These metaphors seem to cast character as a 'thing' – as if it were a constant, palpable thing that we can inhabit, or find, or confront. The more I thought about this, the more it seemed to me that we are getting all these metaphorical ideas wrong. When we play a character, is it helpful to think of that character as being a container, or far away from us, or as someone other than ourselves or as something we must 'master'?

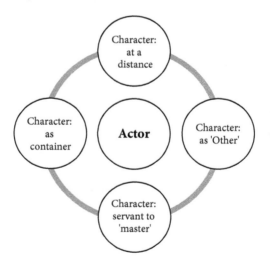

---

[4]Hagen (1973: 152).
[5]Chekhov (1991: 95).
[6]Cole (1983: 79).
[7]Boleslavsky (1965: 77).

I think there are two problems with these metaphors. First, our relationship with whatever character we play must surely have to be deeply intertwined with who we are to begin with. We cannot understand or play Ophelia with someone else's mind – we only have our own to draw on. It seems to me that if we need a metaphor for describing the relationship between actor and character, we might be better off thinking of ourselves as a church organ.

Organs can make a variety of different composite sounds, and organ players heighten some individual sounds and dampen others in order to create the kind of 'sound blend' that they want. They do this by manipulating a series of 'stops' on the organ which they set in order to change the character of the sound it makes.

I think as actors we work in the same way. If we are playing Cleopatra, for example, I think we heighten the parts of us that work best for her and dampen the parts that don't. If we imagine ourselves to have many facets to our character, we can probably immediately imagine which parts of us are suitable for playing Cleopatra. Suppose that we find that at various times we have all of the following aspects to our character:

Controlling	Charismatic	Gentle	Lovable
Flexible	Vulnerable	Strong	Sexy
Energetic	Charming	Realistic	Logical
Agreeable	Confident	Optimistic	Shy
Fair	Cooperative	Organized	Moral
Needy	Kind	Patient	Imaginative
Attractive	Dignified	Honest	Neurotic
Humble	Creative	Heroic	Open
Bitter	Forgiving	Romantic	Funny
Balanced	Generous	Wise	Hard-working
Capable	Intelligent	Careful	Weak
Challenging	Frightened	Mature	Indecisive
Powerful	Self-doubting	Subservient	Quiet
Extreme	Quirky	Opinionated	Loyal

Surely it is likely, then, when playing Cleopatra, we would make the decision to heighten or embody some of these aspects of ourselves and dampen down other aspects of ourselves.

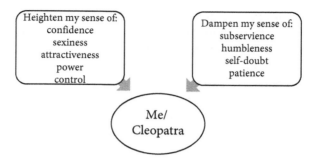

Now as much as I like this idea (because this metaphor of ourselves as an 'organ player' at least keeps the character and the actor together in the same metaphorical space), I am aware that in posing this, I am suggesting that it is the actor who makes all the decisions about which aspects of Cleopatra's character they should heighten or dampen. And this leads to the second problem of the character metaphors, which might be best approached by asking a question.

Who am I anyway?

In my book, *The Philosophical Actor*, I wrote of an exercise that I often do with first-year training actors. I ask them to quickly come up with five words that describe their best friend. They can do this easily – I give them a minute or so and usually watch them silently counting words on their fingers. Then I ask them to come up with five words that describe them. This request *invariably* leads to laughter. Why should describing themselves in five words seem like such a funny idea? After all, they just came up with five words to describe their best friend! When I ask this question, they generally reply that they feel it would be impossible to do such a thing. That might be because they know themselves too well and five words could never cover it. After all – look at the fifty-six adjectives in the chart above – I am guessing that most people have seen moments when their own behaviour could be described in all of these ways. Or perhaps they laugh because it strikes them that they don't really know themselves at all and that, in fact, their behaviour largely depends on context or environment. For example, they might be a social butterfly with a few people and an awkward tongue-tied person with others; they might be confident in some circumstances and completely incapacitated by insecurity in others. They might think they believe one political idea, but quickly switch when they are in the company of some very outspoken or forceful personalities who believe in the opposite idea. Of course, when thinking about ourselves we have a vast interior space to explore. But when thinking about our best friend, we can only explore what we see in their outward behaviour.

However difficult it may be to sum ourselves up in five words, most of us have the sense that WE make the decisions about our own character – after all, who else could be making those decisions? But this idea involves a pretty complicated question:

Do we have anything like a consistent self or character?

This is not an easy question to answer – not only because our 'character' changes in various contexts – but also because even though we have the illusion of a 'self', it is very hard to say of what, exactly, that 'self' is. It might be difficult for us to accept that the 'self' we think of as a consistent thing is an illusion – this is an extremely unpopular idea when I suggest it to my students. Surely, WE know ourselves, don't we? And when it comes to who we are and what kinds of decisions we make, aren't we the ones in the driving seat? Most of my students have argued that the relationship between ourselves and our environment looks like this:

But as most contemporary research reveals, this is an illusion. We do not have a consistent character, and even our sense of 'self' may be no more than a useful illusion.

This conclusion is generally refuted by students, but it is not hard to see why the answer to the question of whether we have a consistent 'self' or character is probably NO. If you have doubts about that, consider these questions carefully:

How does *your own* 'character' change in different places?

- In a bar/pub with friends (*where you might want to be seen as romantic, funny, attractive, sexy, confident, lovable*).

- When you go to a job interview (*where you might want to be seen as flexible, energetic, honest, organized, intelligent, hard-working*).

- When you're online (*where you might want to be seen as extreme, quirky, opinionated*).

How does *your own* 'character' change in different circumstances?

- When you're at work (*where you might want to be seen as organized, logical*).

- When you're at home (*where you might want to be seen as confident, relaxed*).

- When you're at university (*where you might want to be seen as quiet, careful, cooperative*).

- When you need some help in public (*where you might want to be seen as shy, indecisive, kind, cooperative*).

How does *your own* 'character' change around different people?

- When you're with someone you're attracted to (*where you might want to be seen as powerful, sexy, romantic*).

- When you're with your parents (*where you might want to be seen as balanced, confident, mature, organized, careful*).

- When you're with people you don't know (*where you might want to be seen as attractive, intelligent, confident*).

- When you're with people you actively disagree with (*where you might want to be seen as opinionated, intelligent, confident*).

- When you're with people you look up to (*where you might want to be seen as humble, open, kind, wise*).

- When you're with people you look down upon (*where you might want to be seen as powerful, challenging, strong, clever*).

If we think about how profoundly context changes the way that we want to be seen, it is not hard to conclude that environment drives much of our behaviour. The way we wish to be perceived changes our behaviour with various people and in various circumstances and the lists above are all situations where the stakes are not particularly high. When the stakes are high we often change in ways we would not have expected.

If we think about *why* our character changes in each of these circumstances, we will recognize that in every case, what is changing is how we want to be seen in all these various environments. How we want to be seen is not, of course, always connected to what we actually want. In fact, how we want to be seen may differ quite radically from what we actually want. Think about these 'characters':

- **An embezzler:** although the embezzler must set up a system whereby they can quietly steal money, the system will only work if most people see the embezzler as honest, hard-working and loyal.

- **The cheating partner:** although having an affair, the partner will wish to be seen by their spouse as loyal, honest, loving, committed.

- **A drunk driver:** although well over the legal limit, if a drunk is stopped when driving, they must attempt to be seen as sober, responsible, in control.

In fact, the more we think about how our character fluctuates, the more we can see that there is much more involved in terms of our character and behaviour than just some decisions we have made in our heads. Our character is not only changeable, but those changes are also probably the result of at least three things, only a portion of which is decided by us:

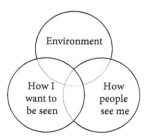

If two of the three elements above are things external to us, we must certainly conclude that much of what we present to the world as our 'character' is generated by the environment around us at any given time. To add to the mix, even the ways in which we want to be seen is very likely have been influenced by external context.

But I think there might be one more thing to consider when we are thinking about our own 'character'. Even if we are fluctuating products of environmental influences, do we not still have some consistent characteristics? Don't we have a history that consists of or creates the 'hidden depths' that drive our personalities? And doesn't this mean that even if we are a bit changeable, we can still predict our own behaviour?

Behavioural scientist Nick Chater would say that all the questions in the paragraph above are 'mirages'. In fact, Chater, in his book *The Mind is Flat*, goes to some lengths to argue that our minds are rather 'flat' in the sense that contemporary research appears to confirm, consistently, that what we think of as 'ingrained' or stable characteristics of our personality are likely to fluctuate fairly wildly under changing circumstances. There is considerable research which demonstrates that:

- we change our views if we find ourselves in a group that thinks differently from us;

- we confabulate (we make up things) in order to ease cognitive dissonance (*cognitive dissonance is the difference between what we might say we believe and what we actually DO believe*);

- we 'improvise' often in social situations, and then justify these improvisations later to ourselves and others.

In fact, it seems that cognitive neuroscientists, social and behavioural psychologists and even developers of artificial intelligence are beginning to realize that we are much more **environmental/ecological** creatures than we are **psychological** creatures: our social responses are not the result of decisions that WE make, but instead are almost entirely generated in response to the environment and circumstances of the moment.

If this is the case, does it make sense for actors to begin from an internal perspective (in which we try to define the character or ourselves)? Surely it makes far more sense for us to focus on environment and to experiment with how we or the character respond/s to that environment. What I am suggesting here is that it might be very helpful for us as actors to rethink our position on acting and the psychology of character and instead of analysing a character we are going to play through classical psychological models (Juliet is rebelling against her mother's authority, Hamlet is secretly in love with his mother), we might be better off basing our analysis on *social* psychology.

The individual is always in a dynamic and changing relationship with the environment around them. The reason this idea is so useful to actors is because a more social analysis of behaviour will help us *shift our focus from self-related thought to thinking much more about what is going on around us*. Not only has research shown that this dynamic relationship can explain much about the ways in which individuals adapt to changing circumstances and environments, it has important added benefits for actors: it keeps our focus external and immediate, it stops us from having all the answers before we start acting and it forces us to pay close attention to how our fellow actors/characters see us, how we want them to see us, how we need them to see us in order to get what we want from them.

Changing our preparation

Clearly, I am suggesting some big changes in the way we approach character, both practically and imaginatively, and that means a rethink of the way that we prepare and the way that we think about character and action. Of course, we are often asked by teachers or directors to prepare a script before we come into a first rehearsal. This seems like pretty standard practice since most directors and teachers in the western world are heavily indebted to the works of Stanislavski. Additionally, most acting books – even the most recent – extend from and are indebted to Stanislavski's writings. If we take just the titles of his work – his first published work was 'Работа актера над собой', which literally translates to 'The Work of an Actor on Himself' – we can begin to see why subsequent actor training has been based, crucially, on the actor building, creating and preparing their work in an individual way.

But along with the idea that we must prepare things before we get to class or to rehearsal, we are also often encouraged to think in terms of 'acting a character' as if we (or that character!) have a sense of a unified and consistent self, with a defined character of sorts, and layers of deep, psychological motivations that we can discover or intuit. As we've seen, we seem to have more than one 'self' – indeed we have multiple selves, and we display them in varying contexts. And the degree of difference between these selves certainly varies. This means that an actor working in isolation on any script can only really discover *some* things.

Predicting behaviour

It seems counter-intuitive, but research has shown time and again that we are incredibly poor at predicting our own behaviour.

Of course, actors have a clear advantage when it comes to predicting behaviour: they know what the characters in a play are going to say and they know what events are going to occur before they happen. But the craft of acting is less about what our characters say or what happens, and much more about how our character behaves and what kind of active choices they make. While we know what Macbeth says and what Macbeth does, we don't know HOW he says or does those things. Most actors have a lot of strategies for creating action and behaviour. Most of them involve the idea that if we look closely at the text (things the character says, things other people in the script say about the character) we can predict behaviour and action. But can we really predict anyone's behaviour? Even our own?

In their influential book *The Person and the Situation*, behavioural psychologists Lee Ross and Richard Nisbett pose a scenario: 'While walking briskly to a meeting some distance across a college campus, John comes across a man slumped in a doorway, asking him for help. Will John offer it, or will he continue on his way? Before answering such a question most people would want to know more about John. Is he someone known to be callous and unfeeling or is he renowned for his kindness and concern? Is he a stalwart member of the Campus Outreach Organization, or a mainstay of the Conservative Coalition Against Welfare Abuse? In short, what kind of person is John and how has he behaved when his altruism has been tested in the past?'[8] Actors, of course, will recognize these kinds of questions, which we use when we are preparing a role. We look to see what kind of things a character values, what their history says about their personalities, and what things other people say about them. This is how we build up the picture of a character we set out to play. But Ross and Nisbett go on to say: 'in fact ... nothing one is likely to know or learn about John would be of much use in helping predict John's behaviour in the situation we've described ... A half century of research has taught us that in this situation, and *in most other novel situations*, one cannot predict with any accuracy how particular people will respond.'

Research in the area of predicting human behaviour has consistently proven that in 'novel situations' such as John's above, intelligence and behaviour respond to environment rather than to any character history or personality traits.

---

[8]Ross and Nisbett (2011: 2; my italics).

Of course, Hamlet's situation is utterly novel (up until Act I, he is a prince studying at university and in love with a young woman whom he is probably going to marry). As research shows, we can be somewhat predictable (even if we fluctuate in different environments all the time) as long as life is routine. But as soon as something dramatic happens (like your uncle murdering your father and then marrying your mother), our behaviour suddenly becomes utterly unpredictable. The reason this matters for actors is that the very nature of drama is to be depicting events that the characters DIDN'T expect. This means characters in drama are probably even more unpredictable in terms of their behaviour or actions. For this reason, we will always be on safer ground working from an analysis of environment than from an analysis of 'character'.

My character wouldn't do that

What if I were to take a step further here and tell you that THERE IS NO CHARACTER? That might seem radical, but given all the research referred to above, it seems that we can never know what our 'characters' will do in novel circumstances. And if we cannot know that, how can we talk about 'character'? A studious and friendly young prince might suddenly become rather paranoid and kill an old man and two of his best friends. A loyal warrior who has led an army to victory on behalf of his king might suddenly murder the king he was being so loyal to. A dutiful young woman might fall for the wrong young man and commit suicide. But crucially, in all of these cases, it *is the audience* and NOT the actor who put together the picture of a character in terms of how they behave, and in terms of the choices they see Hamlet, Macbeth and Juliet making. And this means the actor can't be thinking in terms of 'character'. Instead, the actor is working in wholly unexpected circumstances (Hamlet was not expecting his father's ghost; Macbeth wasn't expecting witches; Juliet wasn't expecting to meet and fall in love with a Montague) and this means that *the actor is attempting to work out how they want to be seen in these unexpected or unknown circumstances.*

In these cases, what is crucial for Hamlet, Juliet and Macbeth is that the people around see them the way that they want to be seen.

And this is where all the pleasure lies for the actor. As Macbeth it is crucial that Duncan see me as his loyal subject when I welcome him to my castle. If I can do this, he will be relaxed, and we will catch him off his guard. As Juliet I must make sure that my mother thinks I am going to take her advice. As Hamlet I must make certain that Polonius thinks I have gone mad. If I do this, he will report my madness to the King, and this will buy me the time I need to think about my next move.

So, if you were the actor playing Macbeth or Juliet or Hamlet in the scenarios above – would it matter what your 'character' was or what your 'character' would ordinarily do? Of course, it wouldn't – the circumstances are so unusual that whatever you might have done in the past will no predictor of what you will do in the present. What would be critical, however, is how you make the other characters see you in order to get a crown, a lover or revenge.

Now, if you put this together with the questions we looked at earlier – how you want to be seen in a variety of different contexts from the pub to a job interview – you might start to realize that what an actor really needs to focus on is not how or what a character IS, but how a character *wants to be seen at any particular moment*.

This not only mirrors the way that we behave in real life, but it also refocuses our thinking from self-related 'character' thinking (default brain mode):

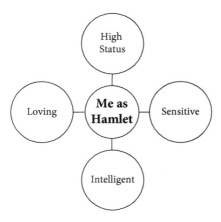

To environment-focused 'action' thinking (task-oriented brain mode):

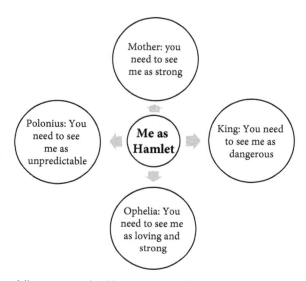

And while we are looking at how Hamlet is responding to his environment, we have to consider the ways in which environment has shaped Hamlet himself. Since his birth, people have seen him as a prince and accorded him the kind of status and power one would expect in that circumstance. No doubt his 'personality' is the result of being fairly secure in knowing that people have seen him as he wanted to be seen: young, next-in-line for the throne, studious, but perhaps a good drinking buddy with close friends like Horatio. whatever it is we make of Hamlet as an individual, we know that he has been shaped by environment, and he will display behaviour that will cause others to see him in the way he wants to be seen. This means that who he is and what he does is entirely the creation of the swiftly changing contexts in which he finds himself.

SUMMARY

1. Putting together a sense of a character is the job of the AUDIENCE and the OTHER ACTORS – *not* the actor's job.

2. Character arises *in the mind of others* based on the choices they see us make. Therefore, for actors, character is revealed in the choices we make as that character but can also change radically if those choices change radically.

3. Contemporary research reveals that when circumstances are new or unexpected, our behaviour becomes unpredictable. As most drama depicts moments in peoples' lives that are new or unexpected, we cannot make predictions about character based on the character's *past* behaviour. That means any time spent by an actor trying to delve into a character's past behaviour can be only partly helpful – and will be most helpful if you remember that unexpected situations bring about unexpected behaviour.

4. Research has demonstrated that we do not know or predict ourselves accurately, and that we are not consistent in our behaviour. Some research even suggests that whatever it is we think of as our 'self' is probably an illusion. Instead, we alter behaviour in response to varying environments: places, people, circumstances.

5. We can think about character as a collection of values and behaviours that may have informed the past, and this will be useful in our preparation for scenes that depict typical contexts for that character. But in extreme circumstances we know that these past values and behaviours may very well be meaningless, and this should be a liberating idea for an actor.

6. As actors, we should always be seeking ways to keep our minds firmly in 'task-oriented' brain mode when we are performing. For this reason, staying focused on how our character **WANTS TO BE SEEN**, instead of what our character **IS**, can keep us focused externally and immediately involved in our imagined environment.

Part Two: How do I use this knowledge in my practice?

Stage One: Preparation

Turn your preparation on its head to keep your options open

Generally, when actors are working on a script by themselves, they rely on convergent thinking to narrow down possibilities. You will want ideas to start with, of course, but remember that convergent thinking at this point can also work against you. Narrowing things down in our preparation can make us miss exciting opportunities that might be afforded to us once we get into a room, working with and watching other people. Other characters 'create' our character, and we 'create' theirs through the ways that we see them and the ways in which they see us. Staying open to opportunities as we work with others means bringing a lot of options into the room. This is the point where we still want to be in using divergent and lateral thinking. If we can do this, we will be alive to all the possibilities that are created in a collaborative art.

The usual preparation looks like an inverted triangle. We seem to begin with observations, then many questions, and then we refine all of that down into some decisions. For example, for an actor playing Hamlet, and thinking about Act III, scene 1, with Ophelia, the inverted triangle might look like this:

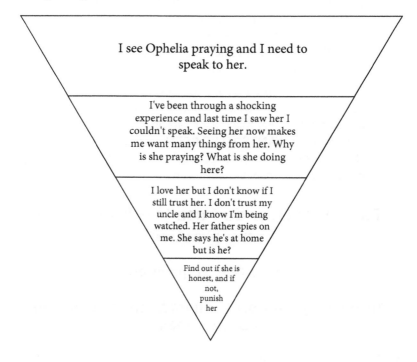

I see Ophelia praying and I need to speak to her.

I've been through a shocking experience and last time I saw her I couldn't speak. Seeing her now makes me want many things from her. Why is she praying? What is she doing here?

I love her but I don't know if I still trust her. I don't trust my uncle and I know I'm being watched. Her father spies on me. She says he's at home but is he?

Find out if she is honest, and if not, punish her

From here, actors are usually advised to attach a list of actions to each line, so looking at my reasoning above I would imagine that the list now will include things like:

I Challenge
I Intimidate
I Disappoint
I Probe
I Ridicule
I Interrogate
I Punish

This list of actions is based on the actor making decisions before they have had much time to see what Ophelia might bring to the scene. It has become standard practice for acting teachers to ask their students to assign an action to every line they have as a preparation for rehearsal. They are usually asked to make this a subject/verb phrase (as above: 'I punish') or simply to write a transitive verb next their lines (transitive verbs can always be preceded by the world 'to', so 'to punish' would work).

While it is perfectly right to say that directors/teachers want actors to bring strong ideas into rehearsal, the difficulty comes when thinking convergently to create a narrow list of verb actions. When you look at the list above once more, you will see there is not much difference between 'challenge', 'intimidate' or 'ridicule'. And there is no difference between 'probe' or 'interrogate' – but I have seen actors work in this way and I have read books that give examples exactly like this in order the help the actor find just the right, fine-grained verb for their specific actions. If we make these action decisions by ourselves, we will almost certainly narrow the field and that is what the inverted pyramid shape above is all about. We go from the broad to the specific.

But what if we turn this inverted triangle on its head, so that rather than a convergent approach, we bring a divergent range of choices/actions/questions to explore with the ensemble? Suppose we go for a model that flips the triangle above, in which we allow the questions to just keep growing, even if they are contradictory? What if we DON'T rule out, and we DON'T narrow down, but instead we keep questioning, based on everything we know about the scene? If we do that, our preparation will look more like this:

I see
Ophelia
praying and
I need to
talk to her

When I saw her last I
couldn't speak. I'm not sure
I trust her, I'm not sure I love
her as I did ... what if she's in
league with the rest and spying
on me? How can I find out just
what is going on with her? Will she tell
me the truth if I just ask her? Why
was she praying here? Does she still love me?

She's giving back my gifts. She looks terribly upset. Maybe
I'll upset her more. How can I find out if she's lying?
Could I try not to give in to my love for her? Can I make
her think I'm crazy? I have to get a message to her uncle.
Can I use her to do that? Will she ever forgive me? She says
her father is at home, but is he? Can I trust her? Is she lying? Shall I
scare her? Although I see she still loves me and I still love
her. I want her to go but does she know I still love her?
Do I care what she thinks? If I do care what she
thinks should I kiss her and then leave? Can I
touch her? Have I scared her? Do I need to hurt her
for hurting me?

Now instead of narrowing down, we are opening out. And once I get into rehearsal, my actions might be:

I challenge
I surprise
I hold her
I push her away
I overwhelm her
I touch her
I laugh at her
I kiss her
I scare her

These actions are much more contradictory and include a much wider range of expression and action for the actor. This opening out also means that a rehearsal process becomes a wide-ranging exploration between at least two actors who can see many possibilities. Until we are working with others, we should not be trying to narrow our options – surely our rehearsals will be richer if we bring more ideas to explore rather than less. If we bring a lot of possibilities into the room, we can then allow the actions and decisions of the actors around us to prompt us into choosing and experimenting with all those possible ideas. We will look closely at this again in the chapter on imagination and intention.

Spend isolated preparation time on environment

The most valuable preparation you can do on your own is on the environment of the play. These kinds of questions can help with this work:

- What is this society? How do people behave here?
- What is rewarded and valued in this community?
- How do I move in these places and what do I wear?
- How do I want to be seen in these places and in this society/community?
- Who are these people and how do I see them?
- How do I want each character to see me?
- What are the sounds of this environment?
- What fills my days and how do I relax in this community or world?

Having some answers to start with here will make your rehearsal contributions valuable to the company.

Stage Two: Rehearsal and experimentation

How being bad can be surprisingly good …

If we bring a lot of possibilities into rehearsal, we eventually start to find the choices that feel right. And as we have seen, choices that we make affect the choices of others and also allow an audience to build their own sense of the character. But as we considered earlier, so much of our self-consciousness arises from the fear of being judged – either by ourselves or by others – for not getting things 'right'. And if we have a sense of what we think is 'right' it must mean that we are also creating a sense for ourselves of what we think is 'wrong'.

As we explore, we narrow down some of these possibilities and the result can often mean that our performance itself gets a bit narrower: less fluid, less open, less dynamic. Along with this we often begin to monitor ourselves more closely from one rehearsal to the next to make sure we are getting things 'right' in terms of what we explored and decided in the last rehearsal. This makes sense, because while you work, you find more concrete and specific actions to play. The challenge is then to make sure that you have not narrowed down your choices in a way that makes you judge yourself as you are performing or relying solely on an intellectual response in creating a performance. The paradox of adequate rehearsal is that it can sometimes make the sense of spontaneous freedom and pleasure in performance disappear.

That means it can be very helpful in this stage to explore what it is you fear or what it is you are worried about getting 'wrong' in your performance or your choices. And while you're doing that, you want to remember that when it comes to art (and to acting), logic is not your only weapon. I see a lot of dull performances that come from actors trying to get it 'right' or trying to be logical. I think trying to be right is the deadliest, because it always proceeds from the fear of being watched, and as we know, that fear creates a self-conscious state of mind.

The very structure of our work tends to make us seek approval – from ourselves, other actors and directors. Too often, actors feel that their work is entirely about getting the reward of praise. The downside of this is that many people become approval-dependent and I do think that many actors find themselves becoming extraordinarily concerned with approval when they work. It is easy to see how this drives a lot of our self-consciousness and fuels some of the endless chatter in our brains while we are trying to focus in performance.

If we consider what I described as 'mental battles' earlier, we can recognize that most of them are driven by the need to be approved and the need to be right. In our need for acceptance and approval, we tend to monitor and flatten our behaviour. We tighten up slightly and watch ourselves carefully, and that generally takes all the pleasure out of an interaction. Think of how your behaviour changes when you meet your partner's parents for the first time or go for a job interview. These situations – where you are very obviously hoping to find approval – seem to make you focus on what you think the parent or the interviewer WANTS from you, rather than just enjoying your conversation seeing how it goes and allowing your responses to arise in a natural way.

For all these reasons, when actors start to tighten and limit themselves in rehearsal, or when the performance is not pleasurable for them, it can help to explore what would happen if they try doing a 'bad' performance. This can be liberating exercise. The idea of working in a way that you know does not need approval can often bring some surprising results, and nearly always has freedom and range in the expression. The only rule of the bad performance is that it must be so bad it makes you laugh. Almost invariably, this direction leads to some surprising discoveries and some interesting work.

The reason a 'bad' performance becomes interesting is that when the actor stops worrying about being right or being logical, the sudden freedom can make a performance exhilarating to watch. Maybe not right – but exhilarating. Sometimes just facing whatever it is we are afraid of will dissipate the fear and allow you to explore more bravely. In so many ways a great acting performance is about letting go. Self-conscious actors make small, tight choices in the hope of controlling things, but great actors trust themselves, let go of control (the 'hypo-egoic' state!) and allow things to happen that they can respond to in exciting, present ways.

You should always plan to get some 'bad' acting into your rehearsal schedule, not only because it helps you figure out what it is you are afraid will be 'wrong', but it also helps to relieve any tightness in your performance. Of course, because you are interfering with holistic memory encoding, you should expect that you will lose text in this exercise, but I believe that it is worth doing and worth having someone on book as you try it. In acting, as in dancing, painting, singing or any other art form, tightness is never good. Flow, ease, openness and adaptability always make for better artistic choices, and allowing yourself to explore what it is you fear will almost always allow you to sense where your performance has grown tight or too careful.

The direction to be 'bad'/'wrong' is a classic double bind: you have been asked (or have asked yourself) to be 'bad', but your ego and desire for approval wants you to be 'good', so whichever way the exercise goes, you win. If your bad performance is, in fact, 'bad' then you did as you were asked (win!). If your 'bad' performance turns out to be 'good', then that is a win as well. Knowing that however it goes you will have done well always brings a kind of freedom into the work that nothing else I have ever tried does. And however it goes, you are almost certain to learn something. Most often in this exercise we find that we are surprised at how well an unexpected approach works and that in itself makes the task worthwhile. But just as often, we find a physical or vocal freedom that was not there before, and it gives the actor something to build on.

Still more important, working this way forces you to disrupt the narrowing effect of convergent thinking and use other tools besides logic in your approach. Some of the best acting performances I have ever seen were good because they surprised me – the actor made choices that I might have thought illogical, then found myself surprised to see that they worked and made me see the possibilities within a scene differently.

For an actor, exploring 'failure' in rehearsal is always interesting when:

1. It makes you laugh.

2. It makes you feel freer, more open and less 'tight' as you work.

3. It brings some unexpected insights into the playing of the scene.

4. It explodes your control of things.

5. It allows you to stop worrying about being 'right'.

6. You learn things from it.

7. It makes the other actors/characters see you differently.

Rehearsal 'failure' is not interesting when:

1. It makes you tighten up.

2. It is monotone or dull.

3. It clings to logic or logical decisions.

4. You stay in control of it.

5. You remain worried about getting 'bad' 'right'.

Inhabit your 'failure' and see where it takes you. It is amazing how often we are not even sure of what it is we are afraid of, and how often trying to control or avoid failure leads us straight to ... failure.

Stage Three: Performance

This is the point where we want to work with our extended mind – remember that character is really a question of how other actors and the audience see you. You might have a strong sense of what your character wants to achieve in a performance, but your success in getting that will depend entirely on how the other actors see you, and on how you make them see you. Your choices here also determine what an audience ultimately puts together as 'your character'.

At this point, if your preparation has been thorough and wide-ranging, you want to be focusing entirely on what is happening around you. Take nothing for granted. Respond to anything that feels even slightly new. Do not assume that what the characters around you did yesterday is what they will do today. Stay focused on discovering what they are thinking about you and exactly how they see you.

If you have spent time within the ensemble exploring all the good and bad options, you should feel comfortable with allowing a range of tactics and choices to enter the performance, even though you know how things will go in the larger sense.

Imagination and attention

Part One: How imagination and attention work

There are a lot of competing theories about imagination. The fact that we do imagine inspires a lot of questions about why we, as humans, should have such an extraordinary and vivid ability to use our imaginative powers to rehearse future outcomes, to mimic the responses of others, to manipulate mental images, to conjure up non-existent worlds or to do so many other things that our imaginations are capable of. There is a reasonable amount of neuroscientific research that explains much about how we create mental images in our imaginations, and there is lot of the research on how imagination develops in child development. This is because imagination figures so heavily in our learning and our lives when we are younger. Most of us can remember the depth of imaginative games we played when we were younger, but many of us struggle to create that kind of imaginative depth once we are adults. This is the challenge, of course, for actors.

When we are thinking about the world of a play or a book as we read, what we are talking about is an imaginative process. This process is called 'fictional immersion' and philosophers and cognitive scientists spend much intellectual labour trying to figure out how it is that we can get so immersed in a fictional experience that we have strong emotional reactions within this immersion. Belief is perhaps the trickiest word to use in this context, because when we are reading an engaging book, is it really the case that the activity involves *belief*? We know, of course, that fictional characters and their circumstances can seem so real that our sense of belief is invoked, but we certainly don't believe that the characters are real in the same way that we believe that our fingers are real. Still, many theorists think that if we do not have some level of belief that Anna Karenina is real, we couldn't possibly find ourselves crying at the ending.

This same question is applicable to theatre, of course, and to the fictional immersion it creates both for actors and audiences. For many years, theatre critics have spoken about the 'willing suspension of disbelief' on the part of theatre audiences. But if we are suspending our DISbelief, then we are necessarily engaging our belief – although only in a kind of 'meta' way. People in the audience are pretending in a way that is actually similar to the actor's process that we considered earlier: they are pretending to forget that they are pretending to believe. And always, in this act of 'pretending to believe', the critical component is imagination.

The difference between real and imagined?

Just exactly how human beings accomplish these different kinds of 'pretendings' is not entirely understood, but we know that we can do these things. If we were able to have a good look at what is going on in our brains when we are imagining things, we might be surprised by what we find there. We might expect that if we had a brain scan while playing Macbeth and imagining that we see a knife floating in front of us, it would look very different from a brain scan taken when we were seeing an actual knife floating in the air in front of us. But in fact, whether the knife is real or imaginary, the parts of our brain that process this information are largely identical. There has been extensive research in this area, and it seems that this holds true for different kinds of imaginings. In one experiment, hearing a real song and then just imagining that we hear a real song later stimulates the same (auditory) areas of the brain. The same is true for seeing a real face and then just imagining the face, which stimulates the same (visual) areas of the brain. Looking at real money excites the orbitofrontal cortex of the brain, and just imagining that you are looking at that money lights up the same area.

This means that when we imagine doing something, we are using the same neurological apparatus that we do when we are actually doing it. But somehow – and this is the tricky part – we know the difference between what is imagined and what is real. We know that when we are pretending to be Juliet, we are pretending. The similarities in the brain response between the real and the imagined *should* mean that we can negotiate the imagined world with some confidence. And yet, as actors, we know how easy it is to interrupt or lose our focused, imagined concentration. This focus can, in fact, be surprisingly fragile. Sometimes it's a dropped line, or a dropped prop. But sometimes – and this is more deadly – it is interrupted by self-consciousness or self-aware thinking (*'this isn't going well'* or *'what is the next line?'*).

The fragile state of attention

This leads us, of course, to the question of attention. In a common sense way, we know how to pay attention to something and we probably also know that while acting, we would love to pay attention only to the imagined world around us. But anyone who has had the experience of acting can tell you that maintaining attention is one of its greatest challenges. This does not only apply to acting – there are many areas in our lives where we struggle to pay attention, and most of us can remember teachers who used the phrase 'pay attention' when addressing us, in the confident sense that what we pay attention to is entirely our choice! But is it? In fact, how we allocate our attention is a highly complex thing, and there are a number of factors that determine our ability to control that allocation.

One of the most interesting studies in this area speaks directly to the challenges an actor can face when attempting to pay attention. A group of researchers gathered people of different age ranges and gave them a task.[1] They were told that while performing the task, a camera would occasionally be turned on (a light would come on so that they would know when) and that they would be watched remotely. The results were that the moment the camera light came on, their brains and bodies exhibited very different patterns than when the camera

---

[1] Summerville (2013).

was turned off. The thought of being watched on camera caused brain patterns to change, and skin conductance (which is a measure of autonomic and not voluntary response) to change, creating the kind of arousal we associate with embarrassment. Neurologist Richard Restak describes how this response to being watched disrupts attention: 'One minute you're concentrating on doing well in the experiment (camera off) and the next moment (camera on) you're concentrating on yourself – specifically, how you will appear to others ...'[2] Clearly, the participants in the research experiment did not CHOOSE to pay attention to themselves suddenly, it simply happened. Which means that the mere thought of being watched switches our attention from an external task to being suddenly aware of ourselves.

It turns out that the very same response happens when we make eye contact – which acting so often requires. A different group of researchers concluded that 'adults' bodily self-awareness becomes more acute when they are subjected to another's gaze'.[3] In neither of these cases would we be able to switch off the brain and body changes simply by trying. The changes were autonomic and not controlled. This goes some way towards explaining why the actor's imagination is so fragile. Interestingly, the first group of researchers found that the strongest responses (which they liken to embarrassment) reached their peak in those at age seventeen. They were markedly less distinct in the very young and the responses 'stabilized' in adulthood. The brain and body changes while being watched were markedly lower in the participants ages six–nine. Perhaps this explains why our childhood imaginations felt so strong?

Two types of imagination

There are many things that can disrupt the actor's fragile imagination, and I think it is important to think about how we can make that focused imagination feel more secure when we're working, and less susceptible to interference. And, as you might have guessed by now, insofar as we can, we want to be employing imagination in the ways

---

[2]Restak (2006).
[3]Baltazar et al. (2014).

that always steer thoughts away from ourselves and securely onto the environment, onto the characters and the world around us. For this reason, we need to be very clear about what type of imagination we are using during the stages of preparation and performance.

However complex the questions around fictional immersion may be, we are still – as actors – involved in a very particular version of fictional immersion (both practical and embodied) when we are acting, but we are using two types of imagination as we do so. It is just as important to recognize how we use these distinct types of imagination as it is to know when we use them.

Type 1 imagination

Type 1 imaginings are all based on intellectual simulations of fictional experiences. They are useful when we are thinking about the world of the play, the events that take place in the play and about what we might imagine the characters are thinking and feeling. We can generally imagine even the most remote circumstance (such as playing a fairy in *Midsummer Night's Dream*) by connecting with memories from our own lives. There are things we may have experienced or felt that might allow us to resonate with things that a fairy may be going through.

You would also use this type of imagination if I asked you to imagine what it would be like to be a cat. Of course, you cannot know from either your own memory or from the cat's experience what it would *actually* be like, but you can still imagine things, yes? If you have a cat, you probably already spend time trying to imagine what the cat is thinking when it meows or rubs up against you or twitches as it sleeps in the sun. This kind of imagination is an intellectual manipulation of various pictures in your mind and possibly various feelings in response to those mental pictures.

For an actor, the imaginative process often begins in default mode by thinking about the character you will be playing and the world they inhabit. For the actor playing Macbeth this might be thinking about (imagining) what he is thinking and feeling:

- **I think Macbeth is thinking …** In this kind of simulation, we are imagining what could be in Macbeth's mind and in classic Stanislavskian terms, this is an 'as if' scenario. So, we try to think 'as if' what has happened to Macbeth has happened to us, and 'as if' we can imagine what Macbeth is thinking. That can only happen once we know who Macbeth is, what his circumstances are, what he wants, what he is afraid of, what he thinks he needs to do, etc., and then we try to answer the question: what would I be thinking if I were in that situation?

- **I think Macbeth is feeling …** In this kind of simulation, we are imagining what kind of emotional responses Macbeth is having in various situations, and as we do in intellectual simulations, we are applying the Stanislavski 'as if' scenario (how would I feel if this were happening to me?). This is also where we might employ Uta Hagen's 'trigger' analysis (what small detail reminds me strongly of how I felt when something similar happened to me?). And we might employ our own unique sense memory (I have been in a cold, dark castle and I've felt those walls, the unevenness of those floors, the enclosed sense of space) or even something as simple as fantasy simulation (what would I feel if I saw a witch on my way home today?). Thought and feeling are deeply intertwined and the work we do on feeling at this stage is not about 'planning' feeling as we act later, but about deepening our resonance with and understanding of Macbeth and his circumstances.

- **I think Macbeth wants …** In this imaginative simulation we are attempting still another 'if' and this time we involve 'prospective imagination' – where we are considering future outcomes. We can see by reading the play that the future Macbeth had originally imagined was as King Duncan's loyal and newly elevated Thane of Cawdor. But the prophecy he hears from the witches has altered that imagined future. He is now considering an imagined future as King himself. But of course, that alone is not enough – we need to imagine what kind of king Macbeth intends to be. Perhaps he has decided that the bloody battles with which the play opens should be stopped: something only the death of Duncan can ensure. Perhaps Macbeth hopes – once his original bloody actions have past – that he can be a king who reigns over a land of peace? There are many ways we might want to imagine what Macbeth wants in the future, and all of them will influence the choices we make in performance.

These Type 1 imaginative simulations are important for deepening our sense of resonance and belief in the imaginary circumstances that we will face when we are performing, and they strengthen and deepen our understanding of what is going on in this imagined world. Type 1 imagination always involves the default brain mode, particularly at the beginning of these kinds of imaginative simulations. This is because default mode is very much centred on your own thoughts and feelings, and we want to start with our own thoughts and feelings. You might want to begin with memories you have of experiences that evoked the feelings of fear, caution and amazement that Macbeth must have felt when he encountered the witches. You might begin with a memory of wanting to have power over something or someone. Default brain mode is involved in autobiographical memories and it works with both slow (using reason and thinking with some effort) and fast (quick, intuitive ideas that 'come to you' rather than you trying to find them) thinking. You might find yourself moving into task-oriented brain mode if you decide that you really want to analyse or research things that might underpin your 'what Macbeth is feeling' or 'what Macbeth is thinking' simulations.

Type 1 imagination kicks in from the moment we first read the play. We might have immediate mental 'pictures' of what Macbeth is seeing when he says, 'So foul and fair a day I have not seen'. We know that he has been victorious in battle, so in that sense the day is fair. But he is now on his way to Forres and it seems that weather is making the journey unpleasant. If you have ever lived in or visited Scotland, you can imagine the kind of weather that Macbeth may be enduring, and some vivid pictures may come to mind.

Along with what we imagine this moment to be like, we also start to imagine the larger circumstances that will affect choices and explorations that we want to make in the preparation and rehearsal stages of our work. Most actors think of what life was like before the dramatic moments that open the play, and what life might be like after.

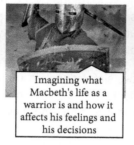

Imagining where Macbeth lives, what his domestic life is like

Imagining what Macbeth's life as a warrior is and how it affects his feelings and his decisions

Imagining how the thought of becoming king might change him and his world

Image credit: Shutterstock.

In terms of our acting work, Type 1 exploratory imagining belongs in stage one, and in stage two, when we are discussing the work in rehearsals, but not in performance.

Type 1 imagination is important for an actor because it is the first step in understanding circumstances and events that create the story and the resonance you might feel with the characters and events. But Type 1 imagination takes place in your mind – it is an intellectual exercise. And as contemporary research reveals, our thinking is produced by more than our brain. To understand this, we might consider what cognitive specialists and artificial intelligence designers call '4E' cognition.

Getting the body involved

'4E' is shorthand for embodied, embedded, enactive and extended, and it is a way of understanding how our bodies play a significant role in shaping and informing what we think. Once we get the body involved in imagination, and when we are actively imagining Macbeth's circumstances at any given point in the play, we can also see how 4E cognition is working:

- Our thinking becomes *embodied*, meaning that what we think is not separate from, but is deeply intertwined with, the environment around us.

- Our thinking is *embedded* within a specific environment, and within that environment we can see opportunities that inspire us to adapt, react and reformulate thought and take action.

- Our thinking is *enactive* in that our actions are always an attempt to make sense of what is happening in an immediate environment. We are also always responding in a natural way and this means that our emotions and the choices we make are inspired by what is going on around us.

- The *extended* cognition of our imagination means that our thinking extends beyond our bodies – to objects and to other people in the environment, which not only form a large part of what it is we are thinking about but also have the power to influence our thinking.

This means that as actors, our most creative thinking happens in the 4E way. We find our most creative and interesting responses when we realize that our thinking is generated not only in our own brains but is also powerfully generated by the environment itself and the opportunities it affords for our reactions, our adaptations and our choices.

Type 2 imagination

I believe the reason that we, as actors, can often find a deep sense of belief in fictional immersion is that *we immerse ourselves in fictional worlds with more than just our brains – we do fictional immersion with our bodies*. It is, no doubt, the body that gives true weight to our sense of belief in ourselves when we are acting. 4E cognition is the result, always, of fluid and dynamic interaction between actors. It allows thought to be generated by that interaction and it means that the interaction becomes the focus of everything.

We begin this 4E thinking when we shift our imagined perspective from Type 1 to Type 2 imagination.

Type 2 imagination is when we are imagining the environment of a scene or event from the character's point of view. This is the moment when we switch our internal mental frame from *thinking* about what it is like to be in Macbeth's body to *being* inside Macbeth's body. When we do this we are changing our perspective from that of an actor thinking about what Macbeth's thoughts and feelings might be, to inhabiting Macbeth's point of view about the events in his world. Others see this more as a switch between two different types of self-projection – where the first is a 'third-person' imaginative projection (I am an outsider, imagining Macbeth's thoughts and feelings), and the second is a 'first-person imaginative projection (I am Macbeth). The theory gets complicated, but the practice is simple: *the switch to Type 2 imagination is what acting is*. Type 2 imagination always involves the task-positive brain mode, and it always involves our body in exploration/simulation:

- **'Is this a dagger which I see before me, The handle toward my hand? Come, let me clutch thee'** ... In this kind of simulation we're imagining that our body is Macbeth's body. We are trying to experience his world physically, so our imagination in this case involves us physically as we grab at the dagger that we're seeing in front of us. Based on whatever ideas we've discovered in our Type 1 explorations and simulations, we are now focusing entirely on the dagger and its meaning. We can 'see' the dagger, and we reach for it. When the dagger disappears, we challenge the reality of it (Is this a trick? Has someone set this up to fool me? Are there people in the shadows watching me?)

- **'Stay you imperfect speakers, tell me more'** ... We're inside Macbeth's body, and we're seeing the witches as he would and watching them carefully. We are balancing a lot of things at once, because in our Type 1 imaginative explorations, we have decided that he must be thinking about the level of danger they represent, whether they are armed or not, whether they are devils, whether they are telling the truth, whether they are trying to frighten him, whether they are real, etc. But whatever I am thinking from inside Macbeth's body here and now, I want to focus on making them talk and tell me more. In order to get this,

I must make them feel that I have the power to hold them here and to make them explain themselves. This means that however impossible it may seem, I must make them see me as a powerful man who is able to command them.

The imaginative work we do in rehearsal alternates between using Type 1 and Type 2 imagination. In rehearsal explorations, we are switching quickly between imaginative types because rehearsals tend to go in stop/start fashion. In the moments where we stop to consider/discuss the work in hand, we are almost certainly stepping back into default mode and engaging our Type 1 imaginations. Once we begin again, we are engaging Type 2 imagination as we work from the perspective of being Macbeth and seeing the world from his physical perspective: we are moving AS Macbeth and not thinking ABOUT Macbeth. So, in this stage, everything we are seeing we are seeing from Macbeth's perspective:

Image credit: Shutterstock.

In performance mode, working through Type 2 imagination exclusively, we have our greatest chance at marshalling and maintaining our attention. It is not that we can suppress the autonomic responses we have to being watched, or maintaining eye contact, because these things will happen, just as our nerves will kick in. But by staying as focused as we can on what is happening around as we immerse ourselves in our Type 2 embodied imaginations, we have the chance of filling up all the mental space available to us in performance. The switch from 'I wonder how Macbeth feels about witches' to 'I have to command these witches' creates a strong external focus that has the power to pre-empt our limited working memory capacity and therefore crowd out the task-irrelevant cognitive activities (like focusing on ourselves or growing self-conscious). Working in this embodied way during stage two and stage three deepens our sense of belief and deepens our text memory. As most actors know from experience, the more you involve your body in an imagined world, the deeper and more focused your imagination becomes. The body 'grounds' and helps to make what you're imagining feel real.

SUMMARY

1. When we are first working – especially in stage one preparation and sometimes in stage two rehearsals, we mostly use our default brain modes. This is because at these points, we are in creative mode: thinking, sometimes daydreaming, calling up our own feelings and memories, and working out various 'as if' strategies.

2. Being watched can seriously impair our ability to maintain focus. This is because the ability to focus attention is only partly in our control. This means we must develop strategies that will help us control what we CAN control.

3. When we are acting – either in rehearsals or performances – we are working in task-oriented brain mode and we are involving 4E, Type 2 imagination only.

4. Type 2 imagination is embodied, embedded, enactive, extended cognition/imagination and these 4E dimensions of the actor-in-the-environment is what anchors us in an imagined world, and allows us to see and respond to that imagined world through a character's eyes. And as always, when we are in full task-oriented brain mode, we are aiming at populating our finite cognitive space with external tasks and details, which helps to limit available space for self-focus.

Part two: How do I use this knowledge in my practice?

Stage One: Preparation

Imagine ideal outcomes before you think in terms of 'verb actions'

If we think about the scene we considered earlier between Hamlet and Ophelia, it is difficult to know exactly what he hopes his ideal outcome with her would be, because at this moment in his life, he can't be sure of much. For this reason, it makes sense that his actions are (as his text is) a bit wild and contradictory. But more often, actors will have a good idea of what their ideal outcome is when they are playing a scene and that ideal outcome is a significant starting place for our work.

Over the last few decades, acting books seem to be recognizing some important things about the nature of our minds, particularly when it comes to the importance of directing our thoughts outward toward the environment and influencing or changing the views of the people around us. You can see this in books like *Viewpoints*, but also in books like Declan Donnellan's excellent *The Actor and the Target*, which encourages actors to think externally about their 'target'.

As we know, whatever it is that the actor chooses in terms of action aimed at their 'target', these choices *become* the 'character' for an audience or the other actors. But how do we know what the right choices are? In our early preparation stage, we are working mostly with the default brain mode – possibly dreaming about how a scene will go or what it means or how it might resonate with memories we have or remind us of people we know. At this point we are not just understanding a script, we are imagining how this script gains meaning to us by examining closely the things that resonate with our own knowledge and experience. And out of this dreaming, we begin the work of imagining the choices we might make in playing the scene.

But rather than choosing an objective that you can phrase as a transitive verb:

I want to frighten you
I want to coerce you
I want to seduce you

I think there is a more complex and exciting way to frame the preparation that you can do before you go into that rehearsal room. Instead of choosing verbs, I think the early preparation needs to involve how you want to be seen and how you imagine the ideal outcome between you and the other characters.

As an example, we can consider the scene between Hamlet and Ophelia, and rather than writing verb actions next to lines, we could create a matrix of the scene that anchors her more securely in our imagination right from the start:

What I want from you	*I want you to be honest and refuse to collude with your father in spying on me. I want you to understand that I have more critical things on my mind than our relationship.*
What is my ideal outcome?	*To avenge my father's death and to make you understand the action I must pursue in order to do this. That you stop being controlled by your father and brother. That you come clean about your father spying on me. That we still love each other.*
How you see me now	*As crazed, emotional, violent, threatening. You think that I am temporarily insane. You might even think you're in danger and that I might harm you.*
How I want you to see me	*As strong. The voice of God. The voice of reason. Your conscience. The person trying to save you from yourself, and from your spying, dishonest father. As strong enough to resist your beauty. As the man you love and who deserves that love.*
How I need to make you feel in order to get what I want	*That our relationship isn't the focus right now. That you've been wrong in spying on me. That you are strong enough to face the truth. That you are loved. That being honest will set you free. Ashamed that you didn't trust me. That beneath it all I still love you. Attracted to me, even in my anger.*

I believe that the right place to start thinking about specific action is in the rehearsal room. But if we frame the action of a scene as above, we not only shift our brain state from self-related thought to task-positive thought, but we also secure the shift from Type 1 imagination (which is a solo act) to Type 2 imagination which is embedded in environment and extended out to include responses to that environment. It keeps us evolving in dynamic, fluid relationships and allows us to take advantage of what happens around us. It means that we aren't tied to one specific action but keeps us focused on how we want to be seen and how we must make other characters feel in order to achieve our ideal outcome.

The important thing here is to remember that we can't get anyone to do anything, unless:

- we know how they see us;

- we know how they are feeling toward us;

- we know what we must make them feel in order to get what we want from them.

We also cannot know how to 'action' something unless we know what our ideal outcome is. And once you have the chance to work with the actor playing Ophelia, you may indeed find that you want to scare her or shame her or adore her, but you will be able to judge even wildly disparate actions in terms of how they suit your ideal outcome. Note that all the answers in the matrix are focused on a person or a situation *external* to the actor playing Hamlet – this helps to ensure that the actor is not sending thought backward, into their own internal space.

Stage Two: Rehearsal and experimentation

Keep attention focused on the impulse to speak

One of the things that often challenges us in early rehearsals is in how we gear our attention toward actively listening, when we have often learned lines as a response to a 'cue' word or phrase. When we learn in isolation, particularly, we tend to learn a line but also the word or phrase that precedes it. You can help to keep your focus on what you're hearing in rehearsal by changing the way you think about 'cue' lines. If you think instead about where the impulse to speak strikes you, not only will you be listening closely to others, but you will also be creating the right tempo or rhythm for a scene. This is sometimes left until later in rehearsal, but because the tempo is so bound up with the learning process, it is best to consider this right from the start of work in rehearsal. Many actors have related experiences of how various directors have tried to influence the pace of a scene, and I have worked with directors who snap their fingers, or simply shout 'pick up your cues'.

But what is it that dictates the pace or the rhythm of a scene? When we work in a company of actors, we know that there is a sense of energy flowing between us. Sometimes we can kind of 'tune in' to that energy and it feels as if the pace of the scene is right. Sometimes we feel as if we are not quite clicking with each other, and the pace of a scene can feel sluggish or not engaging to us.

When we talk about the rhythm of a scene, I think we are really talking about two things: where the actor focuses their attention and where the impulse to speak strikes each actor. Both are important when we are learning because as we know, tempo is part of the holistic experience we learn when we are learning text. When we are watching rather than performing a piece, we can be struck by how quickly it is going. It may feel as if the actors are rushing their lines, or over-energizing to the point where the tempo is rapid and a bit breathless and this, in turn, can make it difficult for us to follow everything that is going on. Sometimes we may be aware of how slowly a piece is going (this has worried nearly every director I ever worked with), and that can often leave us a bit bored in the watching. It seems that tempo is an important part of how we prepare and perform, but it can be difficult to get it right. Of course, it is never a good idea to respond mechanically by simply slowing a scene down or speeding a scene up, since these kinds of mechanical efforts challenge our ability to retain our sense of belief in what we are saying and our desire to represent human behaviour in an organic way. Instead, I think we need to look at what it is in a scene or situation that makes a pause or a quick response the right action.

Some actors affect tempo in a scene by pausing often. Indeed, the 'dramatic pause' is a thing that influences not just the actor taking that dramatic pause but all the actors responding, who are left in a state of limbo until something happens. If you spend a little time observing how this works in real life you will realize that, in general, *there are three places* in a conversation when there are pauses, or where the speakers speak quite slowly:

1. **We may need time to think about how to answer.** This may be because someone has asked a very difficult question. Suppose I were to ask you 'Why does the zero-point energy of the vacuum not cause a large cosmological constant?' Most people would need a little time to come up with the answer to this question. Sometimes we take a lengthy pause if the question demands more information than we are willing to reveal. For instance, someone might ask: 'Are you having an affair?' If the question is coming from your lover and are you ARE having an affair, you will probably need time while you desperately think about how to answer this. In other words, one way to read pauses in dialogue is to assume that the responding actor needs time to figure out how to proceed. Directors rarely worry about taking pauses in situations like this if it is clear that the actor pausing is thinking their way through the situation.

2. **The matter under discussion is not urgent.** For example, someone may say 'I had quite a nice day today'. This is the kind of dialogue that in life would not necessarily even require response, but if the person listening does answer, they are unlikely to feel as if they need to answer this kind of statement quickly, because there is nothing at stake in the statement, and there is nothing at stake in the answer.

3. **Attention may be occupied with something else**. For example, someone may be trying to write an urgent report when asked: 'What would you like to do tonight?' If the

report (or any other difficult business the actor has been asked to do) is consuming their attention, it will take some time to respond. It may also be that when they answer they do so rather slowly as their attention is elsewhere. In a different situation, perhaps someone is occupied in trying to talk to another person out of taking some drastic or dangerous action. In this case the person speaking must be both as calm and as clear as possible. It is therefore likely that in a situation where clarity is important, their attention is on making sure the other person does not miss a word. In this situation, then, the tempo at which they speak might be affected.

When directors want you to go faster, they often mean that in this situation the matter under discussion is more urgent (the stakes are higher) than you think, or it may be that they aren't happy with where you've placed your attention. They might really be asking you to stop directing all your attention to writing that report, and talk to your partner, or they might be suggesting that as important as your talk is with, for example, a would-be suicide, there is something even more urgent on its way and you must hurry.

These are examples where we might think about pausing long enough to think about how to answer or working out just where to place our attention in rehearsal. But I think the more important factor in working out the tempo or pace of a scene has to do with where you feel the impulse to speak.

The messy, everyday impulse

In life when we listen to someone we know when we feel the impulse to speak. That might occur in the middle of their sentence. And we generally know when people we are talking to feel that impulse – we can read it in many ways as we are speaking. They may lean forward or take a breath or raise their eyebrows. Sometimes they just jump in while we are still speaking. The impulse to speak is a strong one and in real life it governs the tempo of all our daily conversations.

Real conversations can be messy and complicated, and a lot of factors contribute to the way pace in constructed. For example, I have a good friend who routinely interrupts me when I speak. When she does, I have learned that it is best to simply allow the interruption. Early in our friendship I would sometimes try to battle it out – carrying on in the attempt to get to the end of my sentence. But I found that she would not stop, even if I carried on, so the two of us would simply be talking at the same time and not listening to each other. I am sure you have watched or been a participant in these kinds of conversations before. We often see them in political debates or family arguments. When the stakes are high, people don't wait politely for each other to finish their sentences.

But as actors, we are given a text and an order in which the characters speak. This means that actors often learn the last word in the line before they speak as their 'cue'. It is this practice, more than any other, I think, that leads us to creating some deadly rhythms on stage and encourages us to focus our attention on the wrong place. Part of what we want to be analysing and practising in rehearsal is determining where the impulse to speak strikes us, and how we negotiate that desire.

It might help to look at an example. The lines below are from *Henry VI*, Part 1 after Joan La Pucelle has been captured. She has been condemned to death by York, Warwick and their army but has asked for mercy as she says she is pregnant. Clearly this is a scene where the stakes are high, and in such circumstances, the impulse to speak is strong and often rather wild. I have marked every place where I think the next character feels the impulse to speak with a § symbol:

Joan La Pucelle: You are deceived; my child is none of his:
It was Alencon § that enjoy'd my love.
York: Alencon! that notorious Machiavel!
It dies §, an if it had a thousand lives.
Joan La Pucelle: O, give me leave, I have deluded you:
'Twas neither Charles nor yet the duke I named,
But Reignier § king of Naples, that prevail'd.
Warwick: A married man! § That's most intolerable.
York: Why, here's a girl! I think she knows not well,
There were so many, whom she may accuse.

As you read this, you can almost hear its rhythm, which is dictated by the fact that the soldiers Warwick and York have been surprised by the fact that the 'saintly' Joan is pregnant out of wedlock. Every name she mentions amazes them, so it is likely that they want to speak/laugh/shout from the moment they hear the names. Having the impulse to speak does not necessarily mean that the actor *does* speak – I think this must be negotiated between the actors/director during rehearsal. But it means that when an impulse is very strong, or strikes early in a line, that lines may overlap. That negotiation may be based on the importance of the information at the end of line. I think in the scene above, the last parts of the line do not give an audience critical information, so when I have directed actors in this scene, where the stakes are very high, I have always encouraged the actors to speak when the impulse strikes them.

This does not always mean that they manage to impede the other actor – often the other actor is aware that someone wants to speak over them, so they grow more forceful in the final part of their line and hold their own right to end. This kind of conversational battle is exciting to watch as long as the scene remains clear to an audience. Many contemporary playwrights have realized that the politeness of actors waiting for their 'cue word' can make a realistic conversation seem dull, so have begun to indicate with a '/' where the actors should jump in as the impulse to speak strikes.

Actors may well change where the impulse to speak strikes them from one rehearsal to the next, because what they hear may be changing slightly at each rehearsal as the actors around them respond to different ideas and challenges. But having to listen closely and think about WHEN you want to speak instead of simply speaking at the end of another actor's line, means that you listen actively and your attention stays in the world happening around you.

When you are in the early phases of working on a scene, ALWAYS look at where the impulse to speak strikes, and never imagine that that last word of another actor's line is the point where you want to speak. It is no exaggeration to say that the energy/pace of a scene is almost entirely dictated by where the actors locate that impulse.

Of course, identifying where the impulse strikes you is also a critical part of the way that you memorize text and performance, so leaving these decisions to the last minute is a bad idea. Just as fiddling around with pace in the last stages of rehearsal is a bad idea. I have known many directors/teachers who ask their actors to do a 'speed run' in the final phases of rehearsal. I confess that this practice has always baffled me, but I long ago concluded that directors who do this must be attempting to create a pressured condition where the actor's memory is challenged in the hope of strengthening that memory.

But as we know, our memories work holistically – they depend critically on the context in which we learned, and that includes pace, movement, action, emotion. So when directors or teachers ask us to do a 'speed run' we are in fact critically interfering with our own holistic memory process.

When it comes to learning the huge amounts of text that we do as actors, there is simply no short cut. We must rehearse until we feel that the basics of our performance – text and movement – have passed into 'automaticity' and require NO effort on our part to retrieve. Until we get to that point, we cannot begin to think about artistry or brilliance in performance.

Attention, imagination and the value of 'boredom'

Years ago, I spent time at the Moscow Arts Theatre school, taking workshops with some of their resident directors. At the end of my time there I saw the run of a production that their students were working on. The director was quick to explain to me that this was a very new production, still in rehearsal, and that the actors had only been rehearsing for six months. When I asked him how long a student company generally worked on a production, he explained that one year was considered the minimum time for student rehearsals.

I was surprised, since at that time (I was working as the Head of Acting at the Royal Central School) we generally gave directors and their student companies four weeks from read-through to first technical rehearsal. I could not imagine our students having the patience to rehearse one production for a year. I spoke with the Russian students after we watched an extraordinarily detailed and engaging run of their production of Alexander Griboyedov's *Woe from Wit*. They were shocked to learn how little time our British students spent in rehearsal and I asked them if they ever grew bored when rehearsing so long. Their answers were a unanimous 'NO'. They described having moments where they felt they had found all they could in rehearsal, and then suddenly discovered things they had never considered, which made all feel fresh to them. They also described the strength of imagination that they brought to the piece, and all felt that six months in, they were secure in the world that they had imagined together and as that imagination strengthened, their concentration grew sharper.

While I do not think that many British acting students would have this kind of patience, I am sometimes surprised at the reluctance amongst young actors to put in even *adequate* rehearsal hours, since being insecure or unprepared are generally listed amongst their greatest fears. I have heard many young actors say that they worry about rehearsing 'too much', and that they feel over-rehearsing will remove the edge of spontaneity or excitement in the work. But perhaps there is something else driving this desire not to rehearse 'too much'.

Very often young actors worry about the way in which rehearsal might compromise their ability to represent emotion. They worry about 'wearing out' their emotional recall by rehearsing too much. This reflects their belief that what is valued in acting is the ability to reproduce emotion. But if you can recognize that your feelings are not a primary concern in the acting process (and certainly should not be the point of your focus), you can stop worrying about this and just be open to allowing the actions of those around you to stimulate any emotional response you may have while performing.

I have also heard actors say that they worry about over-rehearsing because they feel that they have learned all that they need to learn and if they carry on without an audience present, they will start to undo the good work they have done in rehearsal so far and become 'stale'. This also seems a strange reluctance to me, but I have encountered it enough to know that it worries actors.

Although we would find it hard to rehearse a piece for six months, I think we need to do exactly what the young Russian actors were doing – we need to get better at practising through our own 'boredom threshold' and remain patient and deliberate enough in the practice to create and discover new detail and more interesting ways to work in a scene. That kind of practice (even though it occurs in a shorter space of time) is actively securing our own autonomic learning and allowing us the cognitive space to engage in performance with confidence. Once you've worked to the boredom point you will almost certainly have a great security of imagination. Many actors in the profession do six to eight performances a week for a year or more and I am sure I am not alone in remembering that when doing this kind of long run, you tend to go through phases. You sometimes do feel as if you have discovered all there is to discover but creativity is inexhaustible, and the state of boredom has been shown to inspire bursts of creativity. This just might allow you to find things in a performance you had never thought about before.

It sounds counter-intuitive, but in the rehearsal stage of our work *there is value in boredom*. As we know, when we are in the rehearsal phase, we switch often between default and task-oriented brain mode. Boredom can prompt us to unwittingly switch into default, divergent mode, and that is where we find new ideas. Creativity and default mode have been closely linked in research, and you will probably recognize the 'what if' impetus that kicks off a wandering daydream during a boring lecture: what if I were doing something exciting (on holiday, out with friend, at the cinema, etc.). Boredom during rehearsal allows us the same 'what if' exploration: what if I don't try to frighten you but instead make you laugh? What if this isn't about what I thought it was? Boredom can also bring about some lateral thinking – what if we try doing this completely differently?

As long as we don't simply repeat ourselves, boredom in rehearsal can have the same benefit that being 'bad' in rehearsal can have – it stops us from narrowing down options and repeating what we have done before. Instead, it encourages us to open up more questions and to be more courageous in our exploration.

I think the question remains, however: how do we know when we have rehearsed enough to perform? I think we know that we are ready to perform when all the text/movement/thoughts are effortless and require no cognitive energy on our part. This 'automatic' phase means that we are in the optimal state to enjoy performing, and to enjoy interacting with others on stage and feeling secure enough in that interaction to notice when things are slightly different or feeling that sense of energy between you change slightly, and it allows you to enjoy being in front of an audience as well. Until we are at that effortless stage, we are not performing – we are rehearsing.

Stage Three: Performance

Make mindfulness a weapon in your battle to stay focused

Mindfulness can be a significant support to your performance because it can strengthen our fragile ability to maintain attention. There is nothing complex about it – mindfulness is simply the habit of paying attention to exactly what it is you are doing in a given period of time. It is about noticing everything that is happening just in this moment. This sounds simple – and it IS simple – but it surprising how rarely we do it.

Instead, we are quite used to jumping time frames and points of attention and we find our focus scattered during the great majority of our days. We get up and often think about what will happen later in the day. We might cook a meal but listen to the radio or think of a conversation we have just had. Even when talking to people we are often thinking of what we want to say or how they seem different today than they did last week. We share a dinner but sometimes forget to pay attention to the food. To an even greater extent, modern technology has challenged our ability to concentrate. We have grown so used to doing one thing while thinking about another that it can be truly surprising to experience the sensation of focusing on just what we are doing.

The basis of mindfulness is generally described as having five key facets:

1. Observing – this is simply paying attention to what is happening around you at the moment.

2. Describing – this is the act of relating your sensory experience as you look outward.

3. Acting with awareness – this is about purposely paying attention to what is happening at the moment as you take any action.

4. Non-judging of inner experience – this is noting, but not judging, the thoughts that arise in us.

5. Non-reactivity to inner experience – this is letting inner thought and experience simply go without reacting them in any way.

Practising mindfulness

There are several different ways to approach the practice of mindfulness, but most people respond well to the simplest method, which is to focus on an object while breathing 'into' the idea of that object. We can try this now:

1. Choose three objects around you. Anything will do – for our example, let us say a pen, a wall, a desk.

2. You are going to inhale and then think 'that is a pen'. Exhale. While you do this, just look at the pen – if you want, you can notice its colour, shape, texture. Then move your eyes to the wall. Inhale and think 'that is a wall'. Exhale. Again, while you do this, you can simply notice the colour and texture of the wall. You can perhaps imagine how it would feel if you touched it. Next, move your eyes to the desk and as you inhale, think 'that is a desk'. Exhale. Again, you can think about the colour or size or texture of the desk.

3. Stay with this practice and do each object three times, breathing in and out and concentrating just on that object with each breath.

4. If any distracting thoughts arise, observe them, and just let them go. Do not engage with them or think further about them – observe, but do not react.

5. On the second and third repetition, try to slow down the thought 'that is a pen' so that it covers most of your inhalation and exhalation.

This exercise has been referred to as 3 x 3 mindful induction as it very quickly gets you into a place where things slow down, your senses heighten and your concentration feels intensified.

If you have never done simple mindful exercises before these techniques may feel both absurdly simple and strangely profound. We rarely spend time focusing on one simple thing, so the cognitive space that seems open to us when we do can feel immense. Mindfulness is related to meditation and the aim of both is to still the 'chattering' or the 'monkey' mind, which is part of our default mode, and runs away with itself quite often. The more you practise simple, mindful time, the closer you get to finding the strength in stillness and clarity, and in learning to stay with simple, observational and non-judgemental presence. Once you have grown confident with the 3 x 3 exercises above, move onto incorporating mindfulness in the everyday things you do: washing the dishes, chopping vegetables, cleaning or cooking. Simply stay in the present, with these activities, noticing everything that you do.

Daily sessions of this extended mindfulness can combat the habitual 'chatter' of our minds. Much of our self-doubt and self-consciousness inhabit that chattering mind, and over time this chattering mind creates patterns of thought. You may notice that you often say the same phrases to yourself when you are engaged in self-critical thought. Cognitive neuroscientists often use the phrase 'the neurons that fire together wire together' – meaning that when we keep repeating a pattern of neurons that spark a particular thought or behaviour, that pattern becomes increasingly 'fixed', and therefore habitual. They also talk about the 'deep canyons' that we create in our brains that facilitate cyclical and self-defeating thought patterns.

Slowing down into the mindful state creates a kind of circuit-breaker in the default 'chattering' pattern and the more often you can practise mindful concentration, the better you will get in finding that quiet, concentrated space.

During performance, if you can achieve this kind of mindfulness, you will significantly strengthen your ability to stay within the present. With daily practice, you can learn to centre yourself in attention much more effectively.

Affect labelling

Self-conscious thoughts will often spring up when we perform, but there is a simple and important technique that you can try: just give them a label. This is a practice called 'affect labelling', whereby we name whatever it is we are feeling. Simply doing this lessens the effect of the feeling. It sounds too easy to be true, but research bears it out – perhaps the act of stepping back to think about what feeling we're having creates a kind of analytical distance from the feeling? Whatever the reason, research has shown that affect labelling works. The important thing in doing this is simply to observe self-conscious thoughts, name them, and let them go. For example, you may notice: 'that's fear' or 'that's insecurity'. By observing and labelling our feelings we can lessen the intensity of them, so if you observe what you recognize ('my fear', 'my desire to be right', 'my self-critical voice'), you will make a start in weakening its hold on you.

All of these techniques will, of course, knock you out of the ideal external, task-positive performance mode, but with practice they will also help you get back *into* that mode quickly.

Let the performance flow

When it comes to focused attention in performance, the state we are aiming at is flow. Flow is a state first described by Mihaly Csikszentmihalyi – whose work analysed the ways in which athletes and other performers or artists work with a kind of total concentration that feels effortless. Flow state is the result of intensified and sustained attention.

Csikszentmihalyi identifies nine characteristics of 'flow', most of which, it seems to me, describe a good acting experience:[4]

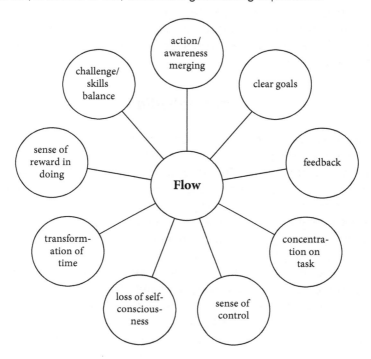

Challenge/skills balance: we need to feel challenged, but not so much that we grow frustrated. The challenge we are attempting as actors needs to match the skillset we currently have and be just a bit beyond that, so we stay engaged. Make sure that you keep increasing the difficulty in terms of what you want to achieve and how you want to change people and situations happening around you.

Action/awareness merging: if we can maintain our focus on those around us and in watching carefully what happens when we play actions or push them into changing their point of view about us or about a given situation, we will create that sense of action and awareness merging together.

---

[4]Csikszentmihalyi (2008).

Clear goals: most actors recognize that they work best when they have very specific goals and actions to play, but as we have seen it helps to keep things fresh and spontaneous if we think in terms of our ideal outcome and then allow our actions to arise in the moment.

Feedback: we need to pay close attention to how our actions are affecting those around us, and we need be in a dynamic, fluid relationship with other actors in order to adjust or change actions in the present moment. If we can't see the impact we are having, it may mean that we need to change tactics.

Concentration on task: we need to build detail and difficulty into our work so that it engages us continuously in the present moment.

Sense of control: the emphasis here is on the 'sense' of control, and this is defined by Csikszentmihalyi as feeling as if you can accomplish anything. This is NOT the same as attempting to control things. But if you can approach a scene with the sense that you are going to win that ideal outcome you will be starting with the idea that you will succeed.

Loss of self-consciousness: this is a big bonus of the flow state – as you become utterly involved in what you are doing, the area of the brain that engages in self-related, self-conscious thought is suppressed. As we have seen, we can't do this by attempting to suppress that thought ourselves, we can only switch our focus to external task-related thinking and that will do the trick for us.

Transformation of time: this is the sense that time is 'flying by' as you work. When we remain immersed in our imagined world, we often feel that a scene goes quickly.

Sense of reward in doing: the flow state generally involves a feeling of satisfaction in the work or feeling as if the work in itself is rewarding.

Emotion

Part One: How emotion works

For some reason emotion has come to have a dominant part in actor training. There are entire schools of thought and training focused on teaching you to emote at will. But the truly curious thing is that when it comes to acting, a show of extreme emotion is very rarely called for. There are times, of course, when a playwright will put something into the text that calls for a show of tears or laughter or anger. Most actors have no difficulty with simulating anger. Many can simulate tears easily enough. Laughter, it is true, is MUCH harder to fake and much easier for an audience to detect when it is faked. But with some exceptions, it is extremely rare for a play or screenplay to require extended laughter. And while watching a great actor conjure up panic or heartbreak might be moving, it is often just as moving to watch a great actor's imagination at work when extreme emotion is not called for. This is because the actor's job is to create the action of the story and in the end, it is the story that moves and engages an audience.

Sanford Meisner once said that if you can conjure up some simulated emotion, fine, use it, but if you can't – just say the lines as truthfully as you can. That advice has always interested me because it seems that what Meisner was saying in the late twentieth century rather flew in the face of so much actor theory and training that had gone before. Indeed, he seemed to be suggesting that the important thing is for an actor is NOT to simulate emotion but simply to convince an audience that they absolutely believe in what they are saying.

In my experience, I find that it is actors themselves who seem to value emotional displays, and that idea often dominates their idea of what acting truly IS. But it would help to think seriously about what it was Meisner was suggesting: which is that emotion is only a small part of what an acting performance involves.

Isn't acting all about emotion?

Emotion and feeling raise a lot of questions for actors, and almost certainly these questions arise out of the fact that acting books (and indeed whole schools of acting) have concentrated so much on emotion/feeling and on how the actor is meant to simulate emotion/feeling truthfully on stage. Stanislavski spent considerable time analysing this and as he explains early in his work, he was always frustrated with what happened when, in his younger years as an actor, he could not force his emotion into play.

Depending on what books you read or what classes you take, much of actor training can centre on emotion/feeling. You might have learned all about emotional 'triggers', 'emotion memory' or 'emotional recall'. You may have been taught or directed by people who speak of having an 'emotional connection' to text or an emotional 'disconnect'. You might even have taken classes that promise to help you access 'truthful emotions' in your acting. But until you understand how emotion and feeling work, none of these things can make sense within the overall practice of acting.

I think the important questions for an actor are:

- What are emotions and how do they differ from feelings? Does this matter for an actor?

- What is the relationship between feeling/emotion and the body?

- How is emotion/feeling generated?

- Is emotion/feeling the same as thought? Can you think *without* feeling?

I think we need to look at all these things before I get around to explaining what this chapter is all about – which is basically this:

Your emotions are none of your business when you are acting.

What is emotion?

This is a far more difficult question than you might imagine. Even for people who make a life out of researching the area, the answers aren't straightforward. Emotion specialist Lisa Feldman Barrett explains that 'an emotion is not a *thing* but a category of instances, and any emotion category has tremendous variety'.[1] The variety of emotions that we feel, the complex ways in which emotions involve our bodies and our minds and the possibility that feeling is related to the ways in which we think about emotion, are all examples of how complex emotion is. This must surely make us wonder how it is that acting books have talked about emotion for so long, without looking more closely at what we mean when we are talking about emotion and feeling.

We seem to use the terms feeling and emotion interchangeably when we are rehearsing and when we are talking about or reading about acting. I often ask actors what they think the differences between feeling and emotion are, and in most cases, they agree that feelings are closer to a thought and emotion is closer to something more primal and involving the body. Feelings are often described as things like insecurity or shyness, whereas emotions are often described as things like fear or disgust or lust. I suppose this is close to what neuroscientist Antonio Damasio was describing when he wrote that emotions 'play out in the theatre of the body', whereas feelings belong to the 'theatre of the mind'. Damasio makes the difference between feelings and emotions very clear: feelings come about when we are trying to make sense of our emotions. And emotions are the physical signals of the body as it reacts to its environment.

---

[1]Barrett (2017: 16).

We do not want to go into anything too complex here (and this is VERY complex territory!), but I think it will help our thinking to agree that emotion is not the same as feeling. Feelings are things like boredom, or calmness, or irritability. Feelings can be pleasant (a little euphoria when you smell your favourite perfume) or unpleasant (the unpleasant feeling when you can't find your car keys and you're going to be late). Scientists generally call this kind of pleasant or unpleasant distinction *valence*. But there is another dimension to feeling called *arousal* which is linked to energy and describes things like how we might feel jittery or 'hyper' when we are about to ask for a rise, or how we might feel tired after a long and difficult argument. We can also talk about energy level when it comes to less physically based feelings – we might become joyful on hearing some good news and this arouses energy. We might grow bored listening to an uninteresting lecture, and this dampens energy.

Emotion, on the other hand, is not a conscious thing. And while it may be risky to hypothesize in such a scientifically controversial area, I think it is safe to say that emotion is something that we do not consciously create – emotion is created for us unconsciously as we navigate our environment. If we see a snake coming towards us rapidly, the incoming sensory data draws together myriad neural responses from different areas of the brain and what we experience is fear. The manifestation of that fear is both quick and unconscious. We do not decide to run when fear takes over us, we DO run. We do not decide to freeze, we freeze. Similarly, when we take the lid off some ancient leftover in the back of the fridge and confront a smelly green mould, we do not decide to feel disgust, we DO feel disgusted. We do not decide to throw up, but we may be throwing up anyway.

These are the ways in which, Barrett explains, 'emotion is meaning' for us: snakes mean danger (and danger means reactions like running or freezing, with all the physiological changes that accompany these actions). Rotten food means disgust (and disgust means immediate dampening of hunger and all the physiological changes that prevent us from eating).

Emotions are closely related to the ways in which our bodies have evolved to make sense of our environment and to secure our survival in that environment. This means that when we talk about 'simulating' emotion we have to remember that we don't create emotion for ourselves in the real world. Emotion involves automatic physiological changes which we cannot evoke by the strength of our own will. This means that trying to simulate true emotional experiences is a complex thing indeed.

While they may be different, emotion and feeling are intertwined with each other, and they connect to thought in a profound way as well. In his book *Self Comes to Mind*, Antonio Damasio asks and answers the question: 'Can there be consciousness without feelings? No.'[2] What he means is that a lot of ideas about how consciousness works (brain vs body; intellect vs feeling) have been fairly thoroughly dismantled by contemporary research. We can't think without feeling. This is one reason why the body is so closely bound up with our thinking process. What we are learning is that the body is part of our thinking process, and that intellectual process is deeply connected with feeling, which itself is deeply connected with the body.

Is thought a 'feeling'?

Despite all the lively scientific debate in this area, I am going to go out on a limb here and say that for our purposes I think what we are usually talking about as actors (when we're rehearsing or performing) is feeling. Since we do not create emotion in the real world, we cannot simulate it easily on stage. We can, however, simulate the *physical manifestations* of that emotion. We can think about what the physical feeling of disgust is like and we can try to simulate the physical aspects of that: we can pretend that our stomach is churning, and our throats are dry and unpleasant. Or we can think about what the physical feeling of fear is like, and we can try to simulate those physical aspects: we can pretend that our hearts are beating fast, that our palms are sweaty and our faces are flushed.

But importantly, as much as we may be able to think about, remember, imagine what an emotion like fear is, we cannot actually *do* the things to our body that fear does by pure will. We cannot make our heart rate speed up. We cannot make our palms sweat, or the hairs on our heads rise slightly, nor make our blood rush toward the surface of our skin by FORCING our bodies to do these things.

---

[2]Damasio (2010: 242).

What we might be able to do, though, is get better at pretending to see something that makes us genuinely afraid. We might be such ace pretenders that we can imagine a spider rushing toward us in such a terrifying way that all those physical symptoms do appear. But that – I would venture to guess – is a pretty rare skill. It depends on an ability to imagine something so deeply that we stimulate some autonomic changes to our bodies. But even if we are great at pretending such things, it will not help us in the middle of a performance to spend time recruiting our fear by imagining a spider, unless the scene we are playing is all about that spider.

For example, suppose in order to simulate Juliet's fear in the crypt, an actor imagines seeing a spider in detail, moving quickly toward her. Such effort would do two worrisome things to the actor playing Juliet: 1) it will send her thoughts backward into her own internal space, knocking her out of the immediate imagined environment in a crypt where she is about to take a scary drug, and 2) it will switch her into self-related thought mode. She will have a task in that self-related mode (vividly imagining a spider), but that task will still isolate her from the imagined world of Juliet in the crypt.

Starting from the body

So, what if we started in an external way, by using our bodies? It seems that there are some ways in which we can sometimes *create* feeling or emotion, but not by thinking about it or imagining things. Specialist Paul Ekman (who has spent decades studying the ways in which faces express emotion and feeling) describes some simple things that we can do physically to 'spark' some feeling. He found that after doing long sessions of imitating facial expressions of sadness or grief, he and his research team began to feel sad themselves. He conducted experiments where he taught people the facial indicators of certain feelings and then monitored them closely.[3] And he found

---

[3]Ekman (2003).

that simply by imitating the facial expression of basic emotions like anger, sadness or fear, the study group did indeed show some physical changes related to the physical responses associated with those emotions.

In these cases, it seems that just creating the facial expression of sadness created a true sense of sadness. You can try this for yourself by looking at the picture below and then following the six instructions afterwards as closely as you can:

Image credit: Shutterstock.

1. Drop your mouth open.

2. Pull the corners of your lips down.

3. While you hold those lip corners down, simultaneously try to raise your cheeks as if you are squinting. This will pull against the lip corners.

4. Maintain this tension between the cheeks rising and the lip corners turned down.

5. Let your eyes look down and your upper eyelids droop.

Research has shown that for most people, a concentrated effort to produce that facial tension evokes an immediate feeling of sadness. it seems that we can sort of initiate some authentic emotion for ourselves – and finding the physical expression of feeling is one way. There is, in fact, a whole training school that will teach you how to invoke feeling by using physical movement and gesture.

But before you embark on that study think about this. In either of the cases above – trying to imagine a spider rushing toward you to cause yourself to feel fear or using the facial muscles in a particular way to express sadness – you will be using concentrated thought that is entirely related to YOU. Either you must focus your thought on attempting to create an imaginary picture of a spider that is real; or you must spend time focusing your thought on rearranging your facial muscles in just the right way to invoke a bit a feeling. Whichever way you go, this is a lot of work, and all of it involves you thinking about yourself and your feelings, and it relocates your focus from the imagined world of a play or scene back on to yourself, opening the floodgates of self-related thought, ideas and doubts.

'Trigger' memories, sense memory, emotional memory

But what about the more traditionally taught ways of helping actors to invoke and then express emotion on stage in a way that feels truthful? Uta Hagen suggests that we distil a memory of some emotional experience down to a small thing that can help feeling flood back into us as we work. Meisner suggested that we prepare ourselves by attempting to relive the memory of an emotion before we start a scene. Many actors use such methods, but we must be pretty disciplined about where and how we use them, because they are only going to be helpful when we want to involve default thinking by imagining various circumstances in which we've felt or experienced something like whatever it is the characters in the play seem to be going through. Without that kind of imagination – empathetic, 'as-if' imagination – we could never relate to the story or the characters, or understand the depth of *their* thoughts and feelings.

But attempting this kind of memory during a performance requires that you temporarily excuse yourself from the task at hand (acting in the present) and involve yourself in a different time frame (representing some mental pictures for yourself from the past).

The WHOLE emotional picture

We tend to begin our work in stage one by thinking about how our character feels. So let's go back to thinking about the kind of work we looked at as preparation work in the Character chapter. Let us say that when we began our work on what Hamlet is thinking and what Hamlet is feeling, we decided that in Act I scene 2 Hamlet is feeling grief at the death of his father, dislike of his uncle and disappointment with his mother's hasty remarriage. And because of all this he might feel a bit alienated from all the people in the new King's court.

Grief
Disappointment with mother
Dislike of uncle
Alienation from the court

Image courtesy of Edinburgh Napier University.

Of course, later when he sees and talks to what appears to be the ghost of his father, he will be adding feelings of fear and perhaps anxiety into the mix of the grief he was already feeling. And those changes of emotion and feeling will proceed through the rest of the play.

Grief

Disappointment with mother

Dislike of uncle

Alienation from the court

Fear

Anticipation

Anxiety

Image courtesy of Edinburgh Napier University.

Actors, directors and acting books approach this kind of analysis differently and there may be many other things to add into these ideas about the kind of emotions that Hamlet is dealing with and what it is that Hamlet is feeling as the five acts progress. But for our purposes, let us start with the emotions we identified in Act I scene 2. As we can see, this gives us very little in terms of what to DO as actors, but it is part of our preparatory thinking.

But of course, we can't confine our consideration here to just what is going on with Hamlet. We need to take the whole environment into account. And to do that, we need to sort emotion/feeling into some useful categories.

Distinctions in emotion/feeling

In his book *Looking for Spinoza*, Damasio suggests some categories of emotion that I think are helpful. The first are **'primary' emotions**, which in Damasio's estimation are things that precede feelings,[4] and these are largely acknowledged to be universal – in other words they are generally cross-cultural and common to all human beings:

The next are what he calls **'background' emotions**. These are the kinds of general *feelings* that we might consult when someone asks us how we are today. Some of the answers might be responding to our levels of hunger, or fatigue or thirst, and they are largely unconscious. But others may arise from specific situations: things that worry us, or annoy us, or make us happy, or content. Although these may not the same as 'mood' (Damasio thinks that moods are longer-lasting) I think we are all right to consider them as moods for

---

[4]Damasio (2004: 29).

our purposes. Thus, we may say of someone that they are in crabby mood or a good mood or a tranquil mood.

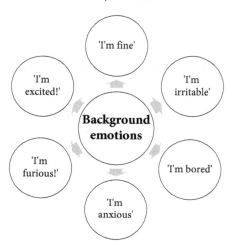

His final category is **'social' emotions** and these are *feelings* that have derived from things we have learned in a social setting. They are the kind of feelings that make most sense if there are other people around. They are connected to other people or the way in which we are perceived by other people. The main social emotions he identifies are:

Once we consider these categories/types of emotions/feelings, it becomes very clear that a LOT of what we feel is generated externally – our primary emotions are generated by our environment, our background emotions *may* be generated by fatigue or hunger or thirst, but just as often they are generated by a good piece of music, or a sunny day or an irritating colleague. And our social emotions are generated by the way we are inspired to perceive others, or how we think they perceive us.

For actors, the important point here is that emotion/feeling is nearly always generated by the world around us, and not by us. This means that if our job is to simulate human behaviour as truthfully and as organically as we can, then our focus must shift from how our character feels to how we can allow feeling to arise naturally in response to what is happening around us.

What are the display rules?

Along with thinking about the types of emotion that might be operating in terms of what Hamlet is feeling, we have to consider what psychologists would refer to as 'display rules' – these are the kinds of social norms that determine what kind of feelings or emotions we can show. This is an interesting category to think about because the 'display rules' change not only in various contexts, and with various people, but also in different cultures. In fact, those changing contexts are somewhat related to what we were looking at in the chapter on Character, when we were considering how our behaviour changes in various circumstances.

Once we consider all these things, we have a far greater sense of what the whole emotional atmosphere of a scene may be, and what might be affecting behaviour at any given moment. Now, instead of this:

Grief
Disappointment with mother
Dislike of uncle
Alienation from the court

Image courtesy of Edinburgh Napier University.

We might have this for Hamlet in Act I, scene 2:

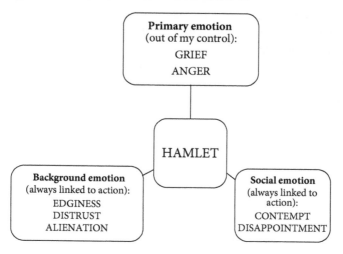

As we know, we cannot control the primary emotions themselves, although we can simulate the physical effects of these. But we have a chance of controlling the display of background and social emotions. We can't 'play' an emotion as that is illogical, so instead we want to make sure that any display of these emotions is tied to action and arises organically. It is important here that the focus remains on the action and not on the feeling. The wider knowledge of this whole emotional picture gives us more precision in terms of how we create and inhabit this imagined world.

Given what we know about Hamlet and where he is in this scene, we also need to know what the display rules are for him. This is helpful in stage one preparation, but we can only do a temporary analysis because we are not in the room, watching what is happening all around us. But we know he is before the King and the Queen so, despite his high status, he is restricted in terms of what he can display. Clearly, he can display his grief (in terms of trying to make Gertrude ashamed for lacking it), and I think he can display his sense of alienation (terms of making Claudius feel unloved and disrespected). Depending on how the actor chooses to play, he might also be able to display some contempt for them (by shaming them for celebrating the marriage), but he would have to be careful, given the circumstances.

Just separating out these kinds of emotions during preparation and rehearsal brings a great specificity to several things for an actor. I think they make clear what parts of the emotional picture are in Hamlet's control and how feeling remains part of action. The work of disentangling emotions and feelings makes clear the relationship between context, character and what can be expressed. We may not be able fully to display our contempt for the King in court, but we can display that contempt fully when playing an action in Horatio's company, where the display rules are more liberal.

Analysing and disaggregating primary, background and social emotion deepens our understanding, and this knowledge is helpful while we are doing our analytical work in preparation and rehearsal. But when we are at the performance stage, we want to be taking in and responding to what we see around us, and this is the point where 'mindreading' becomes much more important to us than what our character is feeling.

Mindreading?

Well, of course, we are not really able to inspect the contents of other peoples' minds. But as philosopher Shaun Nichols points out, we do an ordinary version of this all the time. We are constantly 'reading' each other's thoughts through contextual clues: vocal sound, facial expression, proximity, energy, physical gesture and position. We can think a lot about Hamlet's mind and what he is going through in the early phase of preparation. But we can only know in the most general way how the people around Hamlet are feeling or behaving because we are not in rehearsal room watching them yet. Once we are in rehearsal and performance, Hamlet's feelings do not particularly matter to an actor. They are just useful in determining what Hamlet wants, and knowing what Hamlet wants helps us to determine how Hamlet is going to go about *getting* what he wants.

There are many moments in the play where Hamlet does not seem to know what he wants or what he is going to do next, and these are the great joys and challenges of playing such a complex role. But if we stick with the scene above, we can see that right from the beginning, Hamlet needs to 'read the room' and then also decide what is going on inside the minds of his mother and his uncle. These things will matter enormously when it comes to deciding what kind of action Hamlet wants to take. We may decide that Hamlet's first action is to make his mother feel guilty and to see Hamlet's grief as a kind of threat to her happiness. If I am playing Hamlet, then I might want my mother to see me as slightly threatening. But if Gertrude is looking triumphant and at ease in this moment, and if the whole court of people also look triumphant and at ease, we may have to watch the strength of our action very carefully. We might have to use subtle action that only she might understand and get her to see me as someone she must be wary of. If Gertrude is looking uncertain, and the courtiers look restless and fractious, we might feel that we can be much bolder in the strength of the action we play and kind of energy we put into making Gertrude see us as a threat to her new life with my uncle the king.

In this sense, everything you do as Hamlet depends utterly on everything Gertrude does, and the detailed (sometimes subtle) changes that happen in performance are the things that give actors the chance to keep their performances alive and immediate. For this reason, we don't rehearse to try to get things 'set' – we rehearse to bring the imagined world more and more alive so that when we're performing, we can live securely in that active and fluid world.

I think these things make clear how important it is to see ourselves in performance as dynamic possibility. In life our feelings arise largely in response to how people treat us, and in how we negotiate our way in the world while trying to get what we want/need. We are powerful predicting machines: we predict outcomes and then we adapt when our predictions fail. But in the act of adaptation, many complex thoughts and emotions are generated within us as we attempt to get what we need.

As actors, we want to have a complex 'map' of the primary, background and social emotional possibilities, which will give us greater 'mindreading' and predicting abilities. We also want to have a strong sense of what the display rules are. Not because we must adhere to them at all times, but because there may be great power or advantage in violating those rules just at the critical moments. Great performance comes about when creating feeling/emotion in OTHERS around us. As part a dynamic, fluid and responsive relationship to everything and everyone around us, the creation of feeling in others is how we stay truly attentive and connected to our imagined world. By remaining open and responsive to what others make us feel, we can liberate ourselves from the tedious (and largely impossible) task of trying to generate our own feelings.

SUMMARY

1. Emotion and feeling are different, and emotion is a bodily response to environment that we cannot invoke by ourselves easily. When acting, we are more usually working with feeling.

2. We can try to invoke emotion by simulating the physical manifestations of emotion, but to do so takes our concentration away from the present, so this kind of activity is not helpful when we are in performance mode.

3. In performance mode, we want to stay focused on powerfully influencing the world/the people around us and we need to

allow emotion or feeling to arise from our committed belief in the imagined world around us.

4. There are distinct types of emotion/feeling (primary, background, social) and a clear analysis of all three in the early stages of preparation is helpful for actors and can bring great specificity to both character and context for the performance work.

5. We cannot think *without* feeling and that means when we play an action it will always organically connect with feeling in some measure.

6. It is important to think of performance itself as a dynamic, fluid interplay that is continually interacting with the changing circumstances of the moment.

Part Two: How do I use this knowledge in my practice?

Stage One: Preparation

Using the matrix we looked at in the last chapter, we might now add four boxes at the bottom:

What I want from you	*I want you to be honest and refuse to collude with your father in spying on me. I want you to understand that I have more critical things on my mind than our relationship.*
What is my ideal outcome?	*That avenge my father's death and that you understand the action I have to pursue in order to do this. That you stop being controlled by your father and brother. That you come clean about your father spying on me. That our love survives.*
How you see me now	*As crazed, emotional, violent, threatening. You think that I am temporarily insane. You might even think you're in danger and that I might harm you.*

How I want you to see me	As strong. The voice of God. The voice of reason. Your conscience. The person trying to save you from yourself, and from your spying, dishonest father. As strong enough to resist your beauty. As the man you love and who deserves that love.
How I need to make you feel in order to get what I want	That our relationship isn't the focus right now. That you've been wrong in spying on me. That you are strong enough to face the truth. That you are loved. That being honest will set you free. Ashamed that you didn't trust me. That beneath it all I still love you. Atrracted to me, even in my anger.
Primary emotions	Anger, sadness, disgust (that she would be betray me). **These affect my movement/ physical sense.**
Background emotions	Edginess, desire, suspicion, affection. **These affect the way that I 'read' Ophelia.**
Social emotions	Contempt (for her father), compassion (for the way he controls her), guilt, pride, love. **These affect the tactics I use and the way that I play action as I want to shake her up and make her betray her father.**
Display rules	Anything goes? We have a pretty intimate relationship so there is a wide range of tactics that I can employ, but as I think her father may be listening I might begin by respecting the kind of display a young man would show a young woman when her father is present. By the end, the violation of these rules may help me to achieve my ideal outcome of making you confess your collusion with Polonius' spying.

Again, much will change once you are learning and working with a company, but this analysis will bring you into that rehearsal room with a lot of weapons in terms of analysis and choices open to you. The knowledge that you have once you've spent time creating this matrix is empowering.

Stage Two: Rehearsal and experimentation

Keep feeling linked to action

Action is the organic way to play feeling/emotion. This means that your focus (when you play an action) is always on making the people around you feel something. And in that attempt, the actors around you will be working to make you feel something. Linking feeling to action will always give you the best chance of allowing whatever you feel in the process of acting to arise in an organic way that will not interfere with focus. As you explore different actions you should expect that this will interfere with memory unless you are learning as you explore – which we know is the ideal condition.

Remember that tactics define relationship for an audience

As you explore in rehearsal remember that from the audience's point of view it is the range of tactics that creates relationship between you and the other characters. The closer the relationship, the greater the range of tactics. You can understand this simply by imagining what kind of tactics you use when talking to someone selling you a rail ticket. You will almost certainly keep your tactical choices within the 'polite' range unless the ticket seller is unreasonable. Then you might move into more forceful or authoritative territory. Your physical tactics would almost certainly remain formal, however the exchange goes. Compare this with the way you might try to borrow money from a brother or sister – the physical tactics are likely to vary widely as are the ways in which you play action.

As action, tactics and feeling are all intertwined this means that the range of feeling/emotion that you demonstrate in playing action will similarly define relationships between you and other characters for the audience.

Stage Three: Performance

Learn from Sherlock Holmes

In Arthur Conan Doyle's *A Scandal in Bohemia*, his famous detective explains to Dr Watson the difference between seeing and observing: he points out that although Watson climbs the same set of stairs everyday he is unable to say how many stairs there are. In Sherlock's mind this is the difference between *seeing* the stairs and *observing* the stairs. Holmes, of course, took mindfulness to its extreme.

There is a good reason why our brains don't focus with Sherlock-like attention all the time. As we know, there is limited cognitive processing power and space and if we didn't allow our brains to do some unconscious sifting for us, we would be crowding that space in an unsustainable way. But when we are in performance, the Sherlock laser observation is a state to aspire to.

Rehearsals, like anything repetitive, tend to dull our ability to observe. It takes a positive intention to maintain the desire to see everything anew. It may seem like you and the company are doing what you have done in rehearsal before but as a director I continually observe small changes. And each of these changes signal something about the inner state of the actor.

For example, an actor might usually have sat back in a chair with crossed legs but at rehearsal the next day remains perched on the edge of the chair, or with legs uncrossed. Why? That could indicate a number of things – some of them contradictory. The uncrossed legs seem relaxed, but the forward seating on the edge of the chair seems tense – clearly the character has some struggle in mind or is anticipating something they aren't sure of. Another actor might ordinarily face the person they're speaking to but suddenly turn away or decide to sip their tea at that moment. Why? Perhaps the character has thought more deeply about things and realized that what they are about to say is going to be difficult.

Small changes can give you big clues.

Watch other actors' gestures carefully. When gestures match what a person is saying research has shown that they have a clear understanding of what they are speaking about. When gestures match language inconsistently, it can mean that the speaker is still in the process of understanding a concept or situation that they are talking about. When the gestures don't match the language at all, the speaker may not be very invested in what they are saying or may not even really understand the effect of what they are saying. Observe actors closely when their gestures change.

Monitor proximity – some actors get closer as they get more comfortable. Is this a logical choice where your character is concerned? Have they begun to move further away? Is there something to detect in that change?

Observe props rather than simply 'using' them. What does the delicacy of a china cup say about the person who owns it? What things in the environment are new to your character at that moment and what might these things reveal about the person who owns this environment?

All of these clues give you 'mindreading' powers and keep you intensely focused on what is happening around you in a mindful way. When other actors are confusing you or you find it impossible to 'read' what they are thinking, try a subtle mimic of their body language. Often simply in mimicking what others are doing physically, we not only gain a greater understanding of what they are thinking we can create an unconscious bond between ourselves and them.

Keep your focus continuously on generating feeling in those around you – the more you focus on making them better, more passionate actors, the better and more passionate your work will be.

Performance anxiety

The previous chapters have, I hope, offered some new ideas and advice. But of course, there is a problem with books full of ideas and advice, and it always comes down to one thing: people aren't always in a position to hear/receive that advice.

In this brief final chapter, I want to draw together some important things covered in earlier chapters and look at some techniques to help us avoid the mental battles that sometimes plague our performances.

I have been researching the actor's brain for many years now and I am always surprised at how little research has been done into the area of performance anxiety for actors. There is much written on sports performance anxiety and on music performance anxiety. But there is very little to be found on the performance anxiety of actors. Most seem to assume that where acting is concerned, we will simply get over performance anxiety as we build experience. But this, as we know, is not always true. Some very experienced actors suffer from performance anxiety even after many years of successful performance (in Derek Jacobi's case, he stopped acting altogether for two years due to anxiety although he had been acting professionally for over a decade).

Of course, performance anxiety – or 'stage fright' as it has often been called – is a common part of the actor's mental battle that I see so often. We all recognize the circular ways in which our minds and bodies participate in the performance anxiety mode:

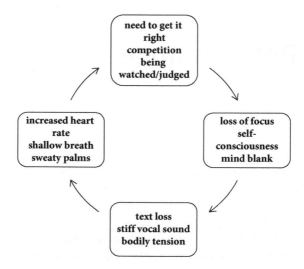

The temptation in these moments is to try to control things, but as we have learned, control is not always the right way to go. Increasingly, research done in this area suggests that we should do the opposite: we should accept what we are feeling instead of trying to suppress or control it. It sounds counter-intuitive, but it seems that if we give up trying to control our anxiety and simply accept it instead, we have a chance of avoiding the circular pattern above.

Your brain is not your friend

Most people are capable of true kindness when responding to others, but we are often unable to be kind to ourselves. Instead, we are tough with ourselves and expect a lot. Some are extremely cruel when judging themselves and frightened of falling foul of that judgement.

Your brain, of course, is not really your friend. If your brain were a person, you would not want to spend much time with it. You can test this idea by comparing what you say to a friend when they do badly in an exam or don't get a job they have applied for, and then thinking about what you say to yourself when this happens. Or perhaps think about what you say to friend who confesses to you that they are insecure about their looks. People will usually find all the ways they can to reassure their friend that they look great and that they should be confident in themselves. But how do you talk to yourself when you feel insecure about your looks? If you are like most people, there is a big difference between the kindness you will show to a friend and the deeply critical ways in which you talk to yourself.

This is where we might want to consider one more facet of default mode thinking: the random and sometimes constant ways in which we criticize ourselves. I believe actors could work in happier, healthier ways if they could stop – or at least significantly lessen – the self-critical, self-conscious 'inner critic' that often haunts us.

The difficult thing about critical self-talk is that research has shown that our brains can't really distinguish whether the talk is coming internally or being directed at us externally – we have the same responses to both internal and external critical judgement. And of course, the rule of the brain is that 'neurons that fire together wire together' – which means that consistent negative self-criticism begins to burn a path in your brain and create habitual dark canyons that you can easily travel through again and again.

Actors aren't like musicians or painters – the instrument they must work through always is themselves. And this means we must spend some time making sure that our whole mental picture is one that will support open, playful and courageous experimentation that allows us to fail and then try again and again.

The power of accepting yourself

What is good enough and is it EVER good enough? Will we ever be completely 'good enough'? And if we are, can we ever know it? Can we ever stop worrying about being 'good enough' and simply concentrate on getting better, and enjoying our own hard work and effort? It seems that we can if we put some effort into it.

Research demonstrates that even a short time spent learning 'compassionate self-talk' makes a significant difference in our mental outlook. Mindfulness practice and self-compassion may seem at first a bit more akin to a self-help website than a book on acting, but increasingly research is finding that there is hard scientific evidence to show the overall benefits of both in terms of mental health and well-being. Both increase our ability to stay present and to win the battle against self-consciousness. This can only be a good thing where acting is concerned.

According to a leading researcher in the area, self-compassion is composed of three things:

1. Being kind toward ourselves rather than critical.

2. Seeing ourselves as part of a wider human experience rather than seeing ourselves as isolated in our failure.

3. Mindfulness, which helps us to observe rather than identify with painful thoughts or feelings.

As I write this, I begin to wonder which book I would recommend to a young actor first: a good reflection on the practice of acting (Donellan? Adler? Merlin?) or a book on self-compassion. Increasingly I begin to think the latter. The ability to accept ourselves and to engage with others in an open and playful way is fundamental to an actor. And that means we need to find a way to observe our negative feelings without identifying with them or seeing our 'failures' as a reflection of our own short-comings.

Along with this I think greater emphasis on self-compassion and training self-talk should be part of an actor's arsenal. This kind of work doesn't take much time, and research has shown positive outcomes from even brief interventions. In one study, participants did two-hour workshops over twelve weeks, and in another, participants did two and a half hours over eight weeks. By the end of both, all participants showed significantly reduced depression, anxiety and self-critical thinking patterns. I can't help wondering whether such training might be just as important for actors as anything else. I am not alone in this conclusion. Music performance anxiety researcher Margaret Osborne has concluded that teaching techniques for coping with performance anxiety would benefit all undergraduate musicians and should form part of their curriculum.

Mindfulness as the basis for so much else

Clearly, the kind of mindful practice that we keep coming back to is an important basis for so much in terms of being able, as an actor, to learn how to stay in the present moment and to keep focused on the things we WANT to focus on. It is also an important part of self-compassion training, and it is an even more important tool for accepting (and not fighting or trying to control) performance anxiety. It is certainly the basis of two important techniques for coping with performance anxiety.

1. 'Grounding mindfulness'

Elizabeth Stanley works with people (many of them post-deployment soldiers) who have experienced trauma. Her techniques have been proven to be powerful for helping people learn to heal and cope with PTSD, and although we are not (I hope!) in that category when it comes to feeling fear or disabling self-consciousness during a performance, I think her grounding technique is really helpful. Essentially, this is much like the 3 x 3 mindfulness technique covered before, but instead of finding three random objects in your view, you focus on a sensory feeling between your own body and the earth or whatever supports you.

For example, if you are standing, you can focus your attention on the solid feel of the ground and the point where your feet come into contact with that solidity. You can simply focus on that feeling while you breath into the observation ('this is my feet on solid ground'). Or you might be sitting and can sense the point where your back, your bottom or the tops of your legs are in contact with the chair or sofa ('this is where I am supported by the chair'). Again, you can breathe into that feeling of being supported. Allow the sense of being supported by the earth or the chair to feel comforting as you breathe.

This kind of mindful awareness is helpful if you suffer much from self-consciousness in performance as it is the basis of what Elizabeth Stanley calls grounding and 'shuttling' technique – which is to alternate between noticing (but NOT ENGAGING WITH) your unwanted self-conscious thought ('my heart is pounding' or 'my hands are shaking') and then alternating that observation with anchoring yourself in the external world (I breathe into the feeling on my feet on solid ground, or I breathe into the sensation of my back against the chair). It may take a few cycles to help you dissipate the unwanted thought but can ease you back into your external world. The important thing about this 'shuttling' is that it provides a physical focus that can stop you from engaging with or worrying about any self-critical thought that arises.

2. Centring process

Developed by performance coach Don Greene, centring is a technique that has been used by athletes and performing artists. I have adapted it slightly for the particular ways in which actors work, and research in both sport and music performance anxiety shows that it is useful in refocusing attention toward performance. Centring for actors could include five steps:

1. Accept that you are feeling nervous. Simply feel it ('that is my heart pounding') and be aware of it.

2. Identify a task: focus on another actor and think: 'I'm going to change the way you see me' or 'I'm going to make you smile'.

3. Feel your physical centre (this can be by breathing into your abdomen) or imagine that you are drawing power from the earth through your legs. This helps to combat the rise of tension in the upper body.

4. Heighten sense: listen very closely, watch something very carefully or better yet, touch something and do it in a 'mindful' way: 'this is cool, smooth and hard to touch. There is no texture but a slight grain from the paint brush' or 'I can feel the tension in your shoulder as I put my hand on it. Your jacket is warm and rough in texture'. The point of this sensory attention is that it can switch your analytical thinking brain into a different, sensory mode which seems to help quiet negative thought patterns.

Letting the mental battle go

Finally, we can always decide to accept our nervousness. This is the big idea behind what is called 'acceptance and commitment therapy'. Instead of struggling with our anxiety, we can recognize that the struggle itself is feeding the anxiety. Some therapists use the act of playing 'tug of war' with their clients. As the client physically struggles with their anxiety (pulling on the rope), the therapist struggles in return. Slowly, the therapist helps to move the client toward seeing that they have the option of just dropping the rope. By 'dropping the rope' and accepting your anxiety, you can decide to let the battle go. Just as in your mindfulness practice, you can learn to observe the thoughts and then let them go. This is why mindfulness practice is so important for performers of all kinds: it helps you to find your still space and simply stay in the present. Remember that we cannot judge a performance with much accuracy while we are in the middle of doing it. We can only judge the quality of our connection with others in an imagined world. Leaving the present to attempt the impossible (accurately judging your own performance and trying to control your performance nerves) is not just counterproductive – it is an act of self-sabotage.

What I am suggesting is that if performance anxiety is a big part of what prevents you from entering wholeheartedly into a joyous exploration of performance, then more books on acting are not likely to help. But there are some great resources that include books and websites on things like mindfulness practice, self-compassion and building resilience and mental strength. While these things are not generally part of the actor training that I am seeing, I wholeheartedly believe that they should be.

Finally ... trust your learning

If you get the learning phases right – if you are memorizing in context and refining, elaborating and encoding thought and action during rehearsals – you will reach the point where the learning becomes autonomic. Imagination will have moved from your mind into your body, and your responses can arise through interaction with others, based on all the preparation you've done. Sports psychologist George Mumford describes the way in which organic, contextualized learning in practice becomes part of the 'adaptive subconscious' – in other words, we have learned by doing things, but we were not thinking explicitly about learning while we did them. We try, we fail and we keep adding to our knowledge and our skills.

This becomes 'implicit' knowledge which we can liken to the way in which we learned to ride a bicycle. We were motivated (we wanted to ride that bike!), we had some knowledge (but we needed to build that through trying), we had immediate feedback (we fell off when we got it wrong) and we kept repeating our effort. But to this day, we are unlikely to be able to explain to anyone exactly how we learned to ride. Good learning – through preparation and rehearsal – should feel like that. And it needs all four elements to make it powerful: motivation, knowledge, feedback and repetition. Even when you are not sure you are making progress, if you keep working through even small steps with these four elements, you will be building your implicit learning.

Performance itself must be based entirely on trust. You have to trust that the careful preparation and learning that you did in the first two stages of the work is solid, and that your retrieval of that work is effortless. Until you can feel that trust, you cannot really say that you are ready to perform. Most actors know this feeling – they know when they have worked with patience and detail to get to the point where they feel ready to have an audience – and in fact are looking forward to that.

At moments when we lose trust in ourselves, we start going backward. These are the moments when we begin to think that *thinking about things* will be helpful. As we have learned, spending time 'reinvesting' thought in things that we already know is not just a waste of time, it will seriously interfere with our ability to perform effortlessly. This is the reason that so much of sports psychology is directed toward getting athletes to just imagine themselves moving with ease and winning. These kinds of visualizations reflect the fact that in the moment of performance, our attention needs to be simply in the moment or on our ideal outcome. When it is time to perform – whether you are an actor or an athlete – you must stay focused on what is in front of you at the moment, and you need to let go of all distraction.

Acting is a complex, fascinating and mostly pleasurable pursuit, and it cannot be hurried. And this means that it is important to remember what we have considered throughout this book, which is learning how to recognize when we are ready to perform.

Performance is a demonstration of the ability to focus on and sustain our engagement in an imagined world.

In the end, perhaps the most important condition for creating a good performance must be faith. This kind of faith comes from trusting in yourself, in your ability to find stillness and clarity in the present, faith in the care you put into the learning and practice of the work, and faith in the strength of the imagined world that you have created with others. This kind of faith allows you to let go of the desire to try to control things.

My aim in this book has not been about helping you to become a GREAT actor – my aim was simply in helping you to become the best actor you can be at the present time by making sure you are in the right cognitive space for exploring your own artistry and imagination. Great acting involves a lot more than we have covered here and requires technical skill that we have not touched on at all.

Instead, throughout this book I have been edging toward trying to answer one question:

What are the ideal performance conditions and how can we create them?

By looking at how our brains think and learn; how the brain focuses differently on the world and on ourselves, I have been trying to explore the knowledge that can help us to create a deep and sustained imaginary state, through which our own responses – either thought or felt – seem natural, organic and believable. Such a state would require as little interference as possible from self-conscious judgement, text insecurity or anything that sends you back into the past. In other words, this state would require that we get *ourselves* out of the way when we perform.

Resources

Along with academic resources below, I want to start this list with some books that were designed to appeal to a popular audience, which means that they tackle some complex areas in an accessible way. These are books I would heartily recommend if you would like to read further about brain, memory, character, imagination, attention, emotion, mindfulness and compassionate mind training.

- Dan Ariely (2010) ***Predictably Irrational*** and ***The Upside of Irrationality: The Unexpected Benefits of Defying Logic at Work and at Home***. London: Harper Collins. *Ariely is a professor of psychology and behavioural economics, but these are not academic books. Instead, they are a fascinating insight into the often counter-intuitive ways in which our brains work.*

- Nick Chater (2018) ***The Mind Is Flat: The Illusion of Mental Depth and the Improvised Mind***. London: Penguin. *Chater is a professor of behavioural science, and his book will almost certainly surprise you. His arguments are persuasive, and the book is enjoyable to read.*

- Bruce Hood (2012) ***The Self Illusion: Who Do You Think You Are***? London: Constable. *Hood specializes in developmental cognitive neuroscience and his book is a well-researched but easy to understand explanation of the ways in which the 'social brain' creates our sense of identity.*

- Annie Murphy Paul (2021) *The Extended Mind*. New York: Houghton, Mifflin, Harcourt. *Murphy Paul has written an extremely well-researched exploration of the ways in which our minds extend well beyond our brains, and of what contemporary research reveals about the best ways to learn and think.*

- Sian Beilock (2010) *Choke: What Secrets of the Brain Reveal about Getting It Right When You Have To*. New York: Free Press. *Beilock is a cognitive scientist who specializes in what makes us tighten up under pressure. This book is a fascinating look at how simple things can dramatically affect performance.*

- George Mumford (2015) *The Mindful Athlete: Secrets to Pure Performance*. Berkeley: Parallel Press. *Mumford is an expert in sport psychology and performance and his book is much more than a look at how mindfulness training can help performance – it's a great meditation on how to live!*

- Kristin Neff and Christopher Germer (2018) *The Mindful Self-Compassion Workbook: A Proven Way to Accept Yourself, Build Inner Strength, and Thrive*. New York: The Guilford Press. *Kristin Neff is a leading researcher in the area of self-compassion and, along with her book you can find an amazing range of helpful (free of charge) resources on her self-compassion website: https://self-compassion.org/.*

- Helga and Tony Noice (1997) *The Nature of Expertise in Professional Acting: A Cognitive View*. London: Lawrence Erlbaum Associates. *Helga and Tony Noice have been researching the role of memory and acting for decades and their work has been influential in many studies of memory.*

Selected bibliography

This is not an exhaustive bibliography, but I have tried to include some further reading for people who want to have a closer look at the research foundations of the book. I have divided these sources into the chapters they relate to.

The actor's brain

Baars, B. J. (1997) *In the Theatre of Consciousness*. Oxford: Oxford University Press.

Brizendine, L. (2007) *The Female Brain*. London: Bantam Press.

Brown, K. W. and Leary, M. (2017) *The Oxford Handbook of Hypo-egoic Phenomena*. Oxford: Oxford University Press.

Buckner, R. L. (2012) 'The serendipitous discovery of the brain's default network'. *Neuroimage* 62 (2): 1137–45. doi:10.1016/j. neuroimage.2011.10.035. Epub 2011 Oct 20. PMID: 22037421.

Buckner, R. L. and Carroll, D. (2012) 'Self-projection and the brain'. *Trends in Cognitive Sciences* 11 (2): 49–57.

Carson, S. (2010) *Your Creative Brain*. San Francisco: Jossey-Bass.

Clark, A. (2010) *Supersizing the Mind*. Oxford: Oxford University Press.

Coates, J. (2012) *The Hour between Dog and Wolf: Risk-taking, Gut Feeling and the Biology of Boom and Bust*. London: Fourth Estate.

Damasio, A. (2010) *Self Comes to Mind: Constructing the Conscious Brain*. New York: Pantheon Books.

Dennett, D. (2005) *Sweet Dreams*. Cambridge, MA: MIT Press.

Doidge, N. (2008) *The Brain that Changes Itself: Stories of Personal Triumph from the Frontiers of Brain Science*. London: Penguin Books.

Eagleman, D. (2015) *The Brain: The Story of You*. Edinburgh: Canongate Books.

Eagleman, D. (2020) *Livewired*. Edinburgh: Canongate Books.

Edelman, G. M. (2004) *Wider than the Sky*. London: Penguin Books.

Gallagher, S. (2005) *How the Body Shapes the Mind*. Oxford: Oxford University Press.

Hassenkamp, W. (2103) 'Using First Personal Reports during Meditation to Investigate Basic Cognitive Experience', in S. Schmidt and H. Walach (eds), *Meditation – Neuroscientific Approaches and Philosophical Implications*, 75–94. New York: Springer.

Kahneman, D. (2012) *Thinking, Fast and Slow*. London: Penguin Books.

Keysers, C. (2011) The *Empathic Brain*. Kindle E-book: Social Brain Press.

Kriss, S. (2017) 'You think with the world, not just your brain'. *The Atlantic*, 13 October.

Langer, E. (1975) 'The illusion of control'. *Journal of Personality and Social Psychology* 32 (2): 311–28.

Leary, M. R., Adams, C. E. and Tate, E. B. (2006) 'Hypo-egoic self-regulation: Exercising self-control by diminishing the influence of the self'. *Journal of Personality* 74 (6): 1803–32. doi:10.1111/j.1467-6494.2006.00429.x.

Masters, R. and Maxwell, J. (2008) 'The theory of reinvestment'. *International Review of Sport and Exercise Psychology* 1 (2): 160–83.

Nalbantian, S. and Matthews, P. M. (2019) *Secrets of Creativity: What Neuroscience, the Arts, and Our Minds Reveal*. Oxford Scholarship Online. doi:10.1093/oso/9780190462321.

Raichle, M. E. (2019) *Creativity and the Brain's Default Mode Network*. Oxford Scholarship Online. doi:10.1093/oso/9780190462321.003.0006.

Ramachandran, V. S. (2004) *A Brief Tour of Human Consciousness*. New York: Pi Press.

Restak, R. (2006) *The Naked Brain: How the Emerging Neuosociety is Changing the Way We Live, Work, and Love*. New York: Harmony Books.

Ritter, S. M. and Ferguson, S. (2017) 'Happy creativity: Listening to happy music facilitates divergent thinking'. *PloS ONE* 12 (9): e0182210. Available online: https://doi.org/10.1371/journal.pone.0182210 (accessed 10 August 2021).

Memory

Anderson, J. R. (2000) *Learning and Memory: An Integrated Approach*, 2nd ed. Hoboken, NJ: John Wiley & Sons.

Bradshaw, G. L. and Anderson, J. R. (1982) 'Elaborative encoding as an explanation of levels of processing'. *Journal of Verbal Learning and Verbal Behavior* 21 (2): 165–74. Available online: https://doi.org/10.1016/S0022-5371(82)90531-X (accessed 10 August 2021).

Conway, M. and Pleydell-Pearce, C. (2000) 'The construction of autobiographical memories in the self-memory system'. *Psychological Review* 107 (2): 261–88.

Damasio, A. R. and Tranel, D. (1993) 'Nouns and verbs are retrieved with differently distributed neural systems'. *Proceedings of the National Academy of Sciences of the USA* 90 (11): 4957–60. doi:10.1073/pnas.90.11.4957.

D'Esposito, M. and Postle, B. R. (2015) 'The cognitive neuroscience of working memory'. *Annual Review of Psychology* 66: 115–42. doi:10.1146/annurev-psych-010814-015031. Epub 2014 Sep 19. PMID: 25251486; PMCID: PMC4374359.

Fernyhough, C. (2013) *Pieces of Light: The New Science of Memory.* London: Profile Books.

Kandel, E. R. (2006) *In Search of Memory: The Emergence of a New Science of Mind.* London: W. W. Norton & Co.

Marois, R. and Ivanoff, J. (2005) 'Capacity limits of information processing in the brain'. *Trends in Cognitive Sciences* 9 (6): 296–305.

Noice, H. and Noice, T. (1993) 'The effects of segmentation on the recall of theatrical material'. *Poetics* 22 (10): 51–67. Available online: https://doi.org/10.1016/0304-422X(93)90020-H (accessed 10 August 2021).

Noice, H. and Noice, T. (1996) 'Two approaches to learning a theatrical script'. *Memory* 4 (1): 1– 17.

Noice, H. and Noice, T. (2006) 'What studies of actors and acting can tell us about memory and cognitive functioning'. *Current Directions in Psychological Science* 15 (1): 14–18. Available online: https://doi.org/10.1111/j.0963-7214.2006.00398.x (accessed 10 August 2021).

Schacter, D. L. (1996) *Searching for Memory: The Brain, the Mind, and the Past.* New York: Basic Books.

Character

Ashton-James, C. et al. (2007) 'Mimicry and me: The impact of mimicry on self-construal'. *Social Cognition* 25 (4): 518–35.

Bond, M. (2014) *The Power of Others: Peer Pressure, Groupthink, and How the People Around Us Shape Everything We Do.* London: Oneworld Publications.

Carter, R. (2008) *Multiplicity: The New Science of Personality.* London: Little, Brown.

Chartrand, T. and Bargh, J. (1999) 'The chameleon effect: The perception-behaviour link and social interaction'. *The Journal of Personality and Social Psychology* 76 (6): 893–910.

Damasio, A. (2010) *Self Comes to Mind.* New York: Pantheon Books.

DeSteno, D. and Valdesolo, P. (2011) *Out of Character: Surprising Truths about the Liar, Cheat, Sinner (and Saint) Lurking in All of Us.* New York: Harmony Books.

Duffy, B. (2019) *The Perils of Perception: Why We're Wrong About Nearly Everything*. London: Atlantic books.

Konnikova, M. (2011) *Don't Just See, Observe: What Sherlock Holmes Can Teach Us About Mindful Decisions*. Available online: https://blogs.scientificamerican.com/guest-blog/dont-just-see-observe-what-sherlock-holmes-can-teach-us-about-mindful-decisions/ (accessed 10 August 2021).

Konnikova, M. (2013) *Mastermind: How to Think like Sherlock Holmes*. Edinburgh: Canongate.

Matz, S. and Harari, G. (2020) 'Personality–place transactions: Mapping the relationships between big five personality traits, states, and daily places'. *Journal of Personality and Social Psychology* 120 (5): 1367–85. Available online: http://dx.doi.org/10.1037/pspp0000297 (accessed 10 August 2021).

McAdams, D. P. (1997) *The Stories we Live by: Personal Myths and the Making of the Self*. New York: Guilford Press.

Meltzoff, A. and Brooks, R. (2008) 'Self-experience as a mechanism for learning about others: A training study in social cognition'. *Developmental Psychology* 44: 1257–65.

Nisbett, R. E. and Ross, L. (2011) *The Person and the Situation*. London: Pinter & Martin Ltd.

Tarvis, C. and Aronson, E. (2013) *Mistakes Were Made (But not by Me): Why We Justify Foolish Beliefs, Bad Decisions and Hurtful Acts*. London: Pinter & Martin Ltd.

Imagination and attention

Agnati, L. F., Guidolin, D., Battistin, L. Pagnoni, G. and Fuxe, K. (2013) 'The Neurobiology of imagination: Possible role of interaction-dominant dynamics and default mode network'. *Frontiers in Psychology* 4: 296. Available online: https://doi.org/10.3389/fpsyg.2013.00296 (accessed 10 August 2021).

Baltazar, M. et al. (2014) 'Eye contact elicits bodily self-awareness in human adults'. *Cognition* 133 (1): 120–7.

Banks, S. (2015) 'Distal and proximal attentional focus effects on the performance of closed and open motor skills'. Doctoral thesis, the University Edinburgh.

Bertolo, M., Filho, E. and Terry, P. (2021) *Advancements in Mental Skills Training*. Abingdon: Routledge.

Bruya, B. and Tan, Y. (2018) 'Is attention really effort? Revisiting Daniel Kahneman's influential 1973 book Attention and Effort'. *Frontiers in Psychology* 9: 1133.

Clark, A. and Chalmers, D. (1998) 'The extended mind'. *Analysis* 58 (1): 7–19.

Csikszentmihalyi, M. (2008) *Flow: The Psychology of Optimal Experience*. London: Harper Perennial Modern Classics.

Dietrich, A. (2004) 'Neurocognitive mechanisms underlying the experience of flow'. *Consciousness and Cognition* 13 (4): 746–61. Available online: https://doi.org/10.1016/j.concog.2004.07.002 (accessed 10 August 2021).

Elpidorou, A. (2014) 'The bright side of boredom'. *Frontiers in Psychology* 5: 1245. Available online: https://doi.org/10.3389/fpsyg.2014.01245 (accessed 10 August 2021).

Harris, P. L. (2000) *The Work of the Imagination*. Oxford: Blackwell Publishing.

Koontz, A. (2019) *The Circuitry of Creativity: How our Brains Innovate Thinking*. Caltech Letters, 12 March. Available online: https://caltechletters.org/science/what-is-creativity (accessed 10 August 2021).

Langland-Hassan, P. (2014) 'What it is to pretend'. *Pacific Philosophical Quarterly* 95 (1): 397–420.

Moran, A. (2009) 'Attention in Sport', in S. Mellalieu and S. Hanton (eds), *Advances in Applied Sport Psychology*, 195–220. Oxford: Routledge.

Nichols, S., ed. (2006) *The Architecture of the Imagination*. Oxford: Oxford University Press.

Parreno, C. and Lønningdal, I. (2020) 'From anonymity to boredom to creativity'. *Architecture and Culture* 8 (2): 275–88. doi:10.1080/20507 828.2020.1792217.

Restak, R. (2006) *The Naked Brain: How the Emerging Neurosociety is Changing the Way We Live, Work, and Love*. New York: Harmony Books.

Summerville, L., et al. (2013) 'Medial prefrontal cortex and the emergence of self-conscious emotion in adolescence'. *Psychological Science* 24 (8): 1554–62.

Tang, Y. and Posner, M. I. (2009) 'Attention training and attention state training'. *Trends in Cognitive Sciences* 13 (5): 222–7.

Watson, G. (2017) *Attention: Beyond Mindfulness*. London: Reaktion Books.

Wells, A. and Matthews, G. (1994) *Attention and Emotion: A Clinical Perspective*. Hove: Lawrence Erlbaum Associates, Ltd.

Emotion

Aviezer, H., et al. (2008) 'Angry, disgusted, or afraid? Studies on the malleability of emotion perception'. *Psychological Science* 19 (7): 724–32.

Barrett, L. F. (2006) 'Solving the emotion paradox: Categorization and experience of emotion'. *Personality and Social Psychology Review* 10 (1): 20–46.

Barrett, L. F. (2017) *How Emotions are Made*. London: Macmillan.

Damasio, A. (2004) *Looking for Spinoza*. London: Vintage Books.

Damasio, A. (2000) *The Feeling of What Happens*. London: Vintage Books.

Ekman, P. (2003) *Emotions Revealed*. London: Weidenfeld & Nicolson.

Ekman, P. (2005) *What the Face Reveals*, 2nd ed. Oxford: Oxford University Press.

Freedberg, D. and Gallese, V. (2007) 'Motion, emotion, and empathy in esthetic experience'. *Trends in Cognitive Sciences* 11 (5): 197–203.

Gladwell, M. (2005) *Blink*. New York: Time Warner Books.

Gross, J. and Barrett, L. F. (2011) 'Emotion generation and emotion regulation: One or two depends on your point of view'. *Emotion Review* 3 (1): 8–16.

Hatfield, E. et al. (1993) *Emotional Contagion: Studies in Emotion and Social Interaction*. Cambridge: Cambridge University Press.

Huther, G. (2006) *The Compassionate Brain*. New York: Trumpeter Books.

LeDoux, J. (1996) *The Emotional Brain*. New York: Touchstone.

LeDoux, J. (2002) *Synaptic Self: How Our Brains Become Who We Are*. London: Penguin Books.

LeDoux, J. (2015) *Anxious*. London: Oneworld Publications.

Panksepp, J. (1998) *Affective Neuroscience: The Foundations of Human and Animal Emotions*. Oxford: Oxford University Press.

Panksepp, J. (2019) 'Emotional foundations of creativity'. Oxford Scholarship Online. doi:10.1093/oso/9780190462321.003.0011.

Pinker, S. (2007) *The Stuff of Thought*. New York: Viking.

Solomon, R. (2007) *True to Our Feelings*. Oxford: Oxford University Press.

Mindfulness, self-consciousness and self-compassion

Baumeister, R. F. (1984) 'Choking under pressure: Self-consciousness and paradoxical effects of incentives on skilful performance'. *Journal of Personality and Social Psychology* 46 (3): 610–20.

Brach, T. (2019) *Radical Compassion: Learning to Love Yourself and Your World with the Practice of RAIN*. London: Penguin Books.

Gilbert, P. (2009) *The Compassionate Mind*. London: Robinson.

Gilbert, P. and Proctor, S. (2006) 'Compassionate mind training for people with high shame and self-criticism: Overview and pilot study of a group therapy approach'. *Clinical Psychology and Psychotherapy* 13: 353–79.

Greene, D. (2002) *Performance Success: Performing Your Best under Pressure*. New York: Routledge.

Hanley, A. W., Mehling, W. E. and Garland, E. L. (2017) 'Holding the body in mind: Interoceptive awareness, dispositional mindfulness and psychological well-being'. *Journal of Psychosomatic Research*. doi:10.1016/j.jpsychores.2017.05.014.

Irons, C. and Herriot-Maitland, C. (2020) 'Compassionate mind training: An 8-week group for the general public'. *British Psychological Society* 94 (3): 443–63.

Juncos D. G. and Markman, E. J. (2016) 'Acceptance and commitment therapy for the treatment of music performance anxiety: A single subject design with a university student'. *Psychology of Music* 44 (5): 935–52. doi:10.1177/0305735615596236.

Kollwitz, M. (2016) 'Breath, tremoring, and performance anxiety: How can Fitzmaurice Voicework's Destructuring address performance anxiety in undergraduate acting training?'. *Voice and Speech Review* 10 (2–3): 100–20. doi:10.1080/23268263.2016.1349726.

Leary, M. and Diebels, K. (2017) 'The Hypo-Egoic Impact of Mindfulness on Self, Identity, and the Processing of Self-Relevant Information', in J. C. Karremans and E. K. Papies (eds), *Mindfulness in Social Psychology*, 5–66. London: Routledge.

Longe, O. et al. (2010) 'Having a word with yourself: Neural correlates of self-criticism and self-reassurance'. *Neuroimage* 49 (2): 1849–56.

Neff, K. D. (2003) 'Self-compassion: An alternative conceptualization of a healthy attitude toward oneself'. *Self and Identity* 2 (2): 85–101. doi:10.1080/15298860309032.

Neff, K. D. (2003) 'The development and validation of a scale to measure self-compassion'. *Self and Identity* 2: 223–50. doi:10.1080/15298860390209035.

Nhat Hanh, T. (1995) *Peace is Every Step: The Path of Mindfulness in Everyday Life*. London: Random House.

Nhat Hanh, T. (2008) *The Miracle of Mindfulness*. Boston: Ebury Publishing.

Niebauer, C. (2019) *No Self, No Problem*. Boerne, TX: Hierophant Publishing.

Osborne, M. S., Greene, D. J. and Immel, D. T. (2014) 'Managing performance anxiety and improving mental skills in conservatoire students through performance psychology training: A pilot study'. *Psych Well-Being* 4 (18). doi:DPI:10.1186/s13612-014-0018-3.

Rochat, P. (2009) *Others in Mind: Social Origins of Self-consciousness*. Cambridge: Cambridge University Press.

Stanley, E. (2019) *Widen the Window: Training Your Brain and Body to Thrive during Stress and Recover from Trauma*. London: Yellow Kite.

Welford, M. (2012) *Building Self-Confidence Using Compassion Based Therapy*. London: Robinson.

Index